KNAPSACK GUIDE
TO
DISNEYLAND® RESORT
PARIS

Look out for other great titles in
the Knapsack Guide Series

Knapsack Guide To London

Knapsack Guide To Brighton & Hove

Get your hands on them and start planning
some more exciting trips!

Where do you think we should do next?
Been somewhere interesting?

Let us know!
hello@knapsackguides.com

KNAPSACK GUIDE TO DISNEYLAND® RESORT PARIS

essential guides for streetwise kids

Written and Researched
by
Michael and Helenor Rogers

Illustrations by Laura Broad

www.knapsackguides.com

Knapsack Guide to Disneyland® Resort Paris

Acknowledgements
Dedicated to everyone who helped us along the
way; with enormous thanks. Especially to our proof readers
(Joanne Gray, Elaine Spindlow, Andrew Osborne, Susie Coyle,
Nicky Kelly and Joan and Brian Rogers) and our supportive
friends and family.

We proudly present the third ever Knapsack Guide.

First published in 2004.   hurrah!
Created, berated and celebrated by Helenor and
Michael Rogers. Cool drawings and cartoons by
Laura Broad.

Photographs kindly supplied by the Walt Disney Company Ltd.
(with the exception of Paris photographs).
© Disney

Proudly Published by Knapsack Publishing Ltd.

Knapsack Publishing Ltd
The Beach Hut
PO Box 124
Hove
BN3 3UY

Printed by the lovely people at Cambrian Printers.

ISBN: 0-9545212-1-8

CONTENTS

INTRODUCTION

So you are going to Disneyland® Resort Paris! You are really lucky, it is the most fantastic place to go. Whether you are into thrill-a-second rides, hysterical shows or enchanting parades there is something for you. As you pass through the Disneyland® Park gates and enter the Town Square you will start to smile, you just can't help it. This place has a funny effect on people... dull, boring grown ups will start to sing out loud and maybe dance a little jig and

NOT JUST FOR LITTLE KIDS

You might be thinking that Disneyland® Resort is just for little kids, but you'd be wrong there. It's a great place for everybody, but especially brilliant if you like fun, action and thrills. Sure, some of the characters are a bit babyish (Chip 'n Dale, Tweedle Dee and Tweedle Dum and the Little Mermaid might not be your thing) but there is plenty other stuff for even the coolest dude in town.

even you will want to wear Mickey Mouse ears. Yep, that's the Disney® magic and you will be dabbed with it.

What did the sea say to the Little Mermaid? Nothing, it just waved!

About This Guide

You will find loads of information about Disneyland® Resort Paris in travel brochures and on the internet and there are other guide books out there, but all written for adults. Unbelievable really, when the people who will enjoy and appreciate this fantastic place the most are kids like YOU.

So we thought it was about time you had your own guide book...

THE UNMISSABLE...

- Space Mountain
    - ✉ Discoveryland©, Disneyland® Park
    - ⓘ See Page 44

- Indiana Jones™ - Backwards
    - ✉ Adventureland©, Disneyland® Park
    - ⓘ See Page 41

- Pirates of the Caribbean
    - ✉ Adventureland©, Disneyland® Park
    - ⓘ See Page 42

- Big Thunder Mountain
    - ✉ Frontierland©, Disneyland® Park
    - ⓘ See Page 40

- The Big Parades
    - ✉ Main St USA©, Disneyland® Park
    - ⓘ See Page 51

- Moteurs...Action! Stunt Show
    - ✉ Backlot, Walt Disney Studios© Park
    - ⓘ See Page 58

- Rock 'n' Roller Coaster
    - ✉ Backlot, Walt Disney Studios© Park
    - ⓘ See Page 56

- Studio Tram Tour®
    - ✉ Production Courtyard ,Walt Disney Studios© Park
    - ⓘ See Page 56

Knapsack Guide to Disneyland® Resort Paris

This guide book tells you what you want to know, not what grown ups think you should know. We cover all the important bits and pieces and lots of other fun stuff with a few jokes and insider secrets too. If you are enjoy boring things like bus spotting and pebble polishing then give this book away to someone else, you probably won't enjoy Disneyland® anyway!

The Layout

The layout is straightforward to make it simple and easy to use. Information is split into 5 main sections:

The Essentials

Takes you through the basic things you need to think about to get the most out of your trip including the best way to get there, how to get around when you are there and importantly, where to find good loos.

The Facts

Gives you a fascinating low down on how the magic of Disney® came about. There is also crucial stuff you didn't even know you needed to know about the park itself, factastic!

Hanging Out

The crucial info. on where it's at and where it's not. There is such a lot to do at Disneyland® Resort Paris, different things that appeal to different kinds of kids - make sure you go to the places that will ring your bell.

The Ultimate

If you just can't be bothered to read all the detail (you'll be missing out...) then head for here, the best the parks have to offer jammed into a day.

Handy Stuff

Does exactly what it says and pulls together useful details such as websites with Disney® info, cash point locations and where to send postcards home.

About Scout

You will find Scout, the alien who has been digging around for you, throughout the book giving you hints and tips and letting you in on his insider knowledge. Scout is <u>the</u> knapsack guide. He also knows million of useful and useless facts and figures. You can find out more about Scout at 🖥 www.knapsackguides.com

What did the alien say to the petrol pump?
Don't you know it's rude to stick your finger in your ear when I'm talking to you!

Think You Know More Than Scout?

If you fancy yourself as a bit of a travel guide then maybe you can help us out? We are always looking for kids to help Scout by providing their views on what's what. All contributors will get a name check in the next book so if you've got something to say get in touch. Contact us on hello@knapsackguides.com.

About 🖥 www.knapsackguides.com

Don't forget to visit 🖥 www.knapsackguides.com for all of the latest info. on Disneyland® Resort Paris. There are also loads of photos, latest timings for the big events and links to useful websites . You can also write to us or post notices so that other knapsackers can see your views – get surfing!!

Warning!

We do try very, very hard at Knapsack Publishing to get things right, but sometimes we make mistakes and other times things change. We can't all be perfect! So if you find something that's not right please tell us about it. Again contact us by email on hello@knapsackguides.com.

Planning Your Activities

Don't turn the page – this isn't just boring stuff that the grown ups go on about. It will make your trip even more awesome - honestly! There are so many choices of things to do at Disneyland® Paris Resort, you will definitely miss out on something you want to

TOP TIPS TO GET YOUR OWN WAY

- First of all set the scene. Be cheerful and enthusiastic about how excited you are to be going to Disneyland®. Adults love that!

- Name drop all of the places that you definitely want to go to. You'll have to do a bit of preparation here (by reading this book – shouldn't be too difficult) so that you know what to mention. Be careful, don't be too annoying.

- Volunteer to organise one of the days for everyone. Ask everyone for their preferences, but sneakily plan the things you want to do.

- Finally, this might be a difficult one... you need to be good, don't make the grown ups cross. Avoid getting stroppy or argumenta- tive, eat all your dinner and don't leave wet towels on the floor. Maybe you could even clean the goldfish without being asked? OK, maybe that's too much!

see or do if you don't plan in advance. You could get someone else to do it, but will they want to do the same things as you? Probably not. A little tedious, but worth it if you want to have the best time ever.

What to Read

We don't recommend reading the whole book cover to cover, dip in and out of the bits you want to read - it's not a story book! If you just want to know what is there for you to do, go straight to the 'Hanging Out' sections. If you would like an idea of a great day out in each of the main parks then head on to 'The Ultimate' and decide on what you fancy doing.

The Day Planners

In 'The Ultimate' we have used a Day Planner (see below) to lay out what to do on the best day ever. Print out extra blank copies of this at 🖥 www.knapsackguides.com.

Day Planner Timed Attractions/Must Do's

What	Where	Start	Finish

What	Where	Notes	

Remember you'll need to be quite flexible as times change, there might also be queues or some things you want to do might be closed.

Web Wandering

For even more information on Disneyland® Resort Paris check out the good old internet. Not only is there stuff on 🖥www.knapsackguides.com but the 🖥www.disneylandparis.com official Disney® site is really comprehensive. Other useful websites are in Handy Stuff at the back of this book.

ESSENTIALS TO TAKE ON YOUR TRIP

- Your passport - you won't get far without it (nice pic eh?)
- Tickets - very, very, very important
- Money - as much as possible, remember to it them into Euros
- A plug adaptor (how else will you charge your Gameboy?)
- Camera - to send us your top pics
- A map (especially if you are going by car)
- A French phrasebook -the basics are included later in here
- A fantastic guidebook (don't forget to pack this one near the top!)
- Weather gear - especially in the winter (it is soooooo cold)

Things to Pack

Even though packing is almost the dullest job ever (only beaten by unpacking), there are a few basic essentials that you need to take with you. Clothes are a good place to start, 'cos it can get a bit chilly in Disneyland® Resort Paris and you might get arrested for walking around naked! On the previous page we've pulled together a quick check list.

What you can get there...

You can buy anything in Disneyland® Resort Paris, there are so many shops selling absolutely everything. That's why you need to earn some extra pocket money for your trip. Shopping is covered in more detail later.

Planning For The Journey

Part of the fun of a holiday should be the journey, although lots of people think it is really boring... they just don't know how to enjoy themselves.

You do need to do a bit of preparation, think about things you will need :

Food and Drink

Sucking sweets, mints, creamy chocolate, crisps, some fruit (apple, grapes, banana), nuts, water (still - fizzy is terrible for burps and other wind...).

Reading Material

Books - this one is a good start. Maybe a magazine - one with puzzles in will kill a few hours, remember a pen. Or how about a book of tricks to annoy grown ups and little sisters?

Gadgets and Games

These times are when Gameboys, Minidiscs or MP3 players (if you are lucky enough to have one) come into their own. Don't forget to charge things up or bring spare batteries. Now you're sorted!

Getting There/ Staying There

There are lots of ways to get to Disneyland® Paris Resort as it is very close to Paris, so the transport links  are excellent. You can fly in, or go by Eurostar train, by coach or by car via the ferry or the Eurotunnel.

Whilst you probably won't be organising the travel, the following info. will allow you to give a bit of advice!

By Air

☎ Roissy-Charles de Gaulle Airport +33 01 48 62 22 80
☎ Orly Airport +33 01 49 75 15 15

If you fly in to Paris you'll probably arrive at one of the 2 airports, Roissy-Charles de Gaulle or Orly, Roissy-Charles De Gaulle is the nearest.

THINGS TO TELL SCARED FLYERS...

Some people are scared of flying, the name for this is 'Aviophobia' or 'Aviatophobia' or 'Pteromerhanophobia'. They would love to be told the following (Not!):

- Did you know we are flying at over 10 thousand metres?
- Don't worry if the engine fails, an aeroplane flying at 10 thousand metres can glide for about 100 miles without power.
- Be careful when you go to the loo, a lady once got vacuum-sealed to a toilet seat after flushing. She only got loose after the aircraft landed.
- If we hit an air pocket we'll only fall a max of 7 metres, it will just feel like a lot more.

Buses from the Airport

☎ Automatic answering information on: +33 01 49 64 47 08
ⓘ Journey takes about 45mins. Pay for your ticket on the bus.
€ Kid's from 3 to 11 years €11,50 (free under 3's)
  Adults: €14
🖳 www.vea.fr

There is a special shuttle service (VEA) connecting both airports with the Disneyland® Resort Paris hotels (except for the Davy Crockett Ranch®). This runs 7 days a week, every 20 mins at peak times and hourly off peak. The buses have 'Disney®' written all over them -  gives you the Disney spirit straight away.

Follow the "VEA Navettes Disneyland® Resort Paris" signs which are in the 'Arrivals' area.

Taxi

Alternatively you could get a taxi, but to be honest, unless there are four of you travelling it probably isn't worth it as taxis are quite expensive (about £60 at time of writing). Also watch out for pretend taxi drivers, they hang about the airport looking for unsuspecting visitors and will rip you off.

By Train

Disney® Express

☎ Eurostar 08705 186 186
🖳 www.eurostar.com

Isn't it amazing, you can now travel right to Disneyland® Resort Paris by train from the UK? The Disney® Express Eurostar service from London Waterloo or Ashford in Kent takes you under the sea, through the French countryside straight to the Disney® doorstep. In only 3 hours from London and 2 hours from Kent!

- Eurostar trains speed along at up to 186mph and generate 1400KW of power, equivalent to 20 Formula One racing cars.
- The trains are 392m long, making them almost as long as a stretched out running track.
- There are 766 passenger seats on every Eurostar train.
- Each train has 48 axles, 96 wheels and 24 bogies (the train undercarriages – not the bogeys you might have been thinking about!)
- Each Eurostar train costs a staggering £24 million!

The train arrives at Marne la Vallée/Chessy station at the gates of the wonderful Disney® Theme Parks. Unfortunately this train doesn't run all of the time, you might need to change trains at Lille in France.

Trains From Paris

If you are staying in Paris or travelling from there you can also take the train. RER line A4 takes you from central Paris (Châtelet-les-Halles Métro) to the heart of Disneyland® Resort Paris in just 40 minutes. Make sure you get on a train that goes all the way to the park (check signs at the station) and get out at the end of the line, Marne la Vallée/Chessy station. Trains stop around midnight.

By Car

Getting to France

There are 2 main options to cross the Channel – by Ferry or by the Eurotunnel train.

DID YOU KNOW?

That the French call the English Channel 'La Manche' which means 'the sleeve'.

The Ferry

There are around 10 ferry routes from England to France, from Plymouth, Poole, Portsmouth, Newhaven, Folkestone and Dover. Dover is the most popular crossing point as it is the shortest route, taking between 70 and 90 minutes.

STOP THE VOM (SEASICKNESS)

- Go on deck and look at the horizon.
- Eat dry crackers and don't drink anything (it just sloshes around in your belly).
- Stay in the middle of the boat.
- Shut your eyes! Having a quick nap is a good idea.
- Hang over the side with a coin between your teeth – well better not, could be dangerous.

What is green, has four legs and two trunks?
Two seasick tourists!

By Eurotunnel

☎ 08705 5 35 35

🖳 www.eurotunnel.com

The Eurotunnel takes you to France in just 35 minutes. You drive on to the train in Folkestone (nearer to the M25 than Dover) and get off at Calais. The carriages are fully enclosed (not that there is much to see in the tunnel) but you can get out and have a mooch around. They have a surprisingly good website with lots of useful info. - take a look!

DIRECTIONS FROM CALAIS...

This is the way to go. Keep an eye on the roads, grown ups have a tendency to go the wrong way.

- Take the A26 motorway (autoroute) heading for Paris / Reims for around 100 km (60 miles).
- Then join the A1 heading south, following signs for Paris.
- Shortly after the Charles de Gaulle Airport, take the next exit onto the A104 motorway follow the signs for "Marne la Vallée".
- After about 27km (16 miles) turn left onto the A4 motorway leading towards "Metz / Nancy".
- Take exit 14 (sortie 14) and then follow signs for 'Val d'Europe, Parc Disneyland®'. or signs for "Hotels du Parc" to head for one of the Disney® hotels.

Driving to Disneyland® Resort Paris

Drive Time

It takes about 3 hours to drive from Dover to the Disneyland® Resort Paris using the motorways, the other roads will add on at least a couple of hours depending on when you travel.

FRENCH FOR DRIVER ASSISTANTS!

- serrez à droite / keep to the right
- à gauche / to the left
- tout droit / straight ahead
- deviation / diversion
- chaussée déformée / uneven road
- ralentissez / reduce speed
- cédez le passage / give way
- essence(sans plomb) / petrol(lead-free)
- stationnement interdit / no parking
- parking gratuit / free parking
- ma voiture est en panne / my car has broken down

Road Rates

Bear in mind that motorways in France cost money, they are called 'toll roads' (autoroutes des péages). You pay by section travelled and it can get expensive, about 50p for every 10km. You can pay by cash, cheque or by credit card. There is always a 'country road' alternative if you like the scenic route.

Parking

There are thousands of parking spaces for day visitors (9,000!- currently €8 a day, just over £5, although it can go up in price if there is a special event taking place). Keep a check on where you are parked, it is labelled by Disney® characters. Then hop on board the moving walkway that takes you towards the parks.

What did Mickey say when Minnie asked if he was listening? I'm all ears!

17

Remember you can't park there overnight and you can park at the Disney® hotels if you are lucky enough to be staying there.

Places to Stay

Where you stay might not be your choice but here is some info. in case the grown ups need a bit of help.

There are lots of options but the most exciting has got to be at one of the seven themed Disneyland® Resort Hotels.

Disneyland® Resort Hotels

The closest hotel is the Disneyland® Hotel overlooking the Park entrance. The rest are situated nearby, around Lake Disney®, with the exception of Davy Crockett Ranch® which is a couple of kms away. They are all really well kitted out in a specific theme, you feel like you are truly living the Disney® experi-

ence. Highly recommended.

REASONS TO STAY IN DISNEYLAND® HOTELS

- Guaranteed access to the Parks, no matter how busy
- Walking distance to the Parks & Disney Village®
- Meet Disney® Characters
- Groovy Disney® Character spoons at breakfast
- Mickey Mouse soaps and shampoos in the rooms
- Shopping is delivered back to your hotel for free!

HIP HOTEL LOW DOWN

● **Disneyland® Hotel ******
The grandest hotel of all; a pretty, pink pleasure palace! The best rooms have a view over Main Street USA® to the beautiful Sleeping Beauty Castle, amazing when it twinkles at night time. A prime spot to watch the parades. Has an indoor swimming pool.

● **Disney's Hotel New York® ******
Luxurious and business-like, with bizarre colours and 'big apples' all around. Groovy views over the Lake, great for the fireworks. Close to the Disney Village® and parks. Has tennis courts, an indoor and outdoor pool and an ice skating rink in winter.

● **Disney's Newport Bay Club® *****
Apparently this is the biggest hotel in Europe, it certainly looks enormous! Decorated with a kind of seaside / boaty theme. Book breakfast in advance, as there are just soooo many people desperate for croissants. Has an indoor and an outdoor pool.

● **Disney's Sequoia Lodge® *****
With a warm, woody décor, this place takes you right back to nature. Like a huge chalet, with a mega stone fireplace where you can toast your tootsies. Groovy indoor and outdoor pools with fab waterslides and hot springs.

● **Disney's Hotel Cheyenne® ****
Walk into the Wild West when you stay here. There are fourteen, brightly coloured buildings that seem to come right from a film set, complete with covered wagons. You check in at the Town Bank and can hang out in the funky Red Garter Saloon.

● **Disney's Hotel Santa Fe® ****
Get down in the desert at the Hotel Santa Fe. You stay in a pretty pastel coloured 'pueblo' amongst bizarre objects like a flying saucer and giant cacti. Has a video games room.

● **Disney's Davy Crockett Ranch®**
A few kms away from the resort, you stay in cute, luxury log cabins or you can pitch up a tent right in the middle of the forest. Lots to do; pony rides, face painting, basketball, karaoke, archery and swimming in the tropical pool. You do need a car as there is no bus service provided, but you can park for free.

FIND NEMO...

Check out the fish tank by the restaurant downstairs at Disney's Newport Bay Hotel...see if you can spot Nemo hiding...

Other Hotels

There are other hotels nearby with more being built; some brill, others boring, boxy, business places. You could also stay in the centre of Paris and travel in by train, or stay in a nearby town like Meaux or Fontainebleau and drive in. Many package holidays include hotels, you don't even have to think about it.

Getting Around

From the Disneyland® Hotels

You can walk to the Disney® Theme Parks past the lake to the Disney® Village, (takes 20 mins) or take the free shuttle buses that leave every few minutes.

From the Station

The Marne la Valee station is right outside the gates of the both parks, and next to the Disney® Village. Hop on the escalator out and walk through the gates!

Maps

There is a map of the whole of Disneyland® Resort Paris on the inside front cover of this book (and of the two parks in "Hanging Out"), but we recommend that you pick up a map from the entrance as you come through the gates, they also have the latest timings.

The maps are very pretty but are a little deceptive; the place isn't as huge or as complicated as it looks.

GET LOST!

It is quite likely that you will get lost in the Disneyland® Park, less likely in the Walt Disney Studios© Park - but don't panic... pretend it is a bit of an adventure:

- Look up and try to locate the bright pink Sleeping Beauty Castle, make your way towards this central point.
- Look out for signs or one of the rides / attractions and then locate this on your map.

- Agree an emergency rendezvous spot with the others you are with – for example if someone is missing everyone makes their way to the Streetcar Stop in Central Plaza.
- There is a lost children meeting place near the Plaza Gardens Restaurant and First Aid stop in the Disneyland Park® and in the Front Lot in the Walt Disney Studios© Park.
- Think about taking Walkie Talkies with you. They are quite cheap nowadays and are great fun as well as being useful.
- Ask one of the cast members for help... they wear an "i" on their costumes will happily help you out or answer any questions!

Getting Your Bearings

Remember there are two separate parks, the Disneyland® Park and the Walt Disney Studios© Park. Depending on your ticket you may be able to go to both or may be restricted to one. If you can go to both fantastic, do it. If not we would recommend sticking to the Disneyland® Park, it is much bigger and has more things to see and do.

Disneyland® Park

This is divided into 5 imaginary lands.
- Main Street USA®
- Frontierland®
- Adventureland®
- Fantasyland®
- Discoveryland®

You enter through Main Street USA® and then the lands follow around with the Central Plaza at the centre, as you might have guessed.

I NEED A WEE

Sometimes you just have to go – now! Luckily the loos in the parks are generally clean and easy to find! There can be quite long queues during the Summer when it gets busy, so go whenever you have the opportunity!

Loo Locations
- By the City Hall
- By the Buggy / Wheelchair Pick Up
- By the Coffee Shop / Ice Cream Shop on Main Street USA®
- Next to the legends of the Wild West, Frontierland®
- To the left of the Fuente del Oro Restaurante, Frontierland®
- Just before the Indiana Jones™ Backwards! ride, Frontierland®
- Next to Aladdin's Bazaar, Adventureland®
- By the Fantasyland® station
- By the Discoveryland® station
- Next to Autopia, Discoveryland®
- In / by some cafés e.g. Silver Spur Steakhouse, Cowboy Cookout Barbecue, Au Chalet De La Marionnette, Pizzeria Bella Notte
- Disney® Village – not nice loos, grubby, tatty, scabby – YUKKKK!!

Walt Disney Studios© Park.

This is divided into four easy to get around areas:
- Front Lot
- Production Courtyard
- Backlot
- Animation Courtyard

The entrance is through the Front Lot studios.

The Essentials

TRANSPORT FOR TIRED FEET!

Sometimes you need a rest, try out the other transport options!
These are available in the Disneyland® Park

● Disneyland® Railroad,
Take the cute tooting train to get an idea of where things are and
to pick out your 'must visit' places. The train stops at
Frontierland, Fantasyland and Discoveryland so if you want to go
to Adventureland you're stuffed! Actually Adventureland is only a
short stroll from the Frontierland station so it's no big deal.

● Main Street Vehicles
Maybe being chauffeur driven down Main Street is more your
thing? You can choose between the perfectly reproduced Paddy
Wagon, Omnibus, Limousine or Fire
Engine, the more lazy original way to
travel. Thumb a lift at the Town
Square and Central Plaza.

● Horse-drawn Streetcars
For a special treat, trot on down
Main Street on board the beautiful
tram pulled along by stunning
Percheron horses. Climb aboard at
Town Square or at Central Plaza.

Getting Around the Parks

Walking Around

Walking is a great way to get around and is really your
only choice so wear comfy shoes. In the Disneyland®
Park it will take you about 5 minutes to walk from Skull
Rock in Adventureland to Big Thunder Mountain in
Frontierland, and about 20 minutes maximum to go
from one side of the park to the other. The Walt
Disney Studios© Park is even easier to walk around,
taking less than 15 minutes to go from end to end.

Useful Info

Tickets / Passports

☎ 08705 03 03 03
🖥 www.disneylandparis.com
ⓘ Costs c.€30 kids/ €40 adults per day

If you've not bought a package deal then you need to think about what kind of ticket you'll need.

Remember Disney® classify kids as under 12's - does that mean 12 yrs + are adults? Certainly means you'll pay the adult price 'though doesn't mean you can drink at the bar...

TICKET TIPS

- **1 Day Theme Park Ticket**
  Provides admission* to either Walt Disney Studios© Park or Disneyland® Park.
  Can exit and re-enter that same Park as many times as you wish.
  If you spend the day in Walt Disney Studios© Park, your 1 day ticket also entitles you to "Disneyland® Park Evening Access" letting you enter Disneyland® Park 3 hours prior to its closing.
  Must be used within 3 years - (see date on back of ticket).
  * subject to Disneyland® Park capacity

- **2 Day Disney Parks Hopper Ticket**
  Allows total freedom between the 2 Theme Parks as often as you wish during the 2 days.
  2 days do not need to be consecutive but must be used within 3 years - (see date on back of ticket).

- **3 Day Theme Parks Hopper Ticket**
  Allows total freedom between both Parks as often as you wish during 3 days.
  3 days do not need to be consecutive but must be used within 3 years - (see date on back of ticket).

  Tickets allow unlimited, free access to attractions, shows and parades (excluding the Shooting Gallery in Frontierland© and the Video Games Arcade in Discoveryland© in Disneyland® Park and the Halloween Parties.

You can get 1 day, 2 day and 3 day tickets - Disney® call them passports. Each have there own rules and regulations so you need to understand what you can do!

Fastpass Frenzy

Fastpass is a great Disney® invention - a way to skip the queue without everyone going mad at you! Check out what rides offer this (most of the big ones) and go there first. Stick in your 'passport' and get your 'raffle' ticket with your allotted time on it. The just return to the ride in your time slot and get into the short Fastpass queue - delightful!

Opening Hours

🕐 Daily, 9am until 11pm in summer, 10am until 8pm in winter

The parks are open 365 days a year – even Christmas Day, how cool is that? The opening hours depend on the season, and then sometimes vary within this just to make it even more confusing! It is best to check the closing time as you walk into the parks, there is a sign by the gates. If you need to know before you go check out 💻 www.disneylandparis.com.

EARLY DOORS

Although the official opening time is 9am / 10am you can usually get in at least ½ an hour earlier. Whilst the rides and things won't be open you can wander around and get to the front of the queue, especially important in the summer.

Also be careful 'cos in the summer if it gets too busy they will not let anyone else in (except resort Hotel guests – handy tip!). Disney® Village stays open late, even past midnight if you get to stay up super late.

The Weather

Weather by time of year

The table below shows the weather you can expect in Disneyland® Resort Paris, but be prepared. You are also likely to have really bright sunny days in February and pouring wind and rain in August, not much different to the UK. You would have thought they could have built it somewhere nice and sunny... but then it wouldn't be so close to home!

	J	F	M	A	M	J	J	A	S	O	N	D
Avg. Max (°C)	6	7	11	14	18	21	24	24	21	15	9	7
Avg. Min (°C)	1	1	3	6	9	12	14	14	11	8	4	2
Mean (°C)	4	4	7	10	14	17	19	19	16	12	7	5
Rainfall (mm)	46	39	41	45	56	56	57	55	53	56	54	49

The 'Mean' doesn't mean nasty or stingy – it is the overall average temperature for that month. 'Avg. Precip.' means average precipitation which is just a fancy word for 'wet stuff'; rain or snow to you and me.

PUBLIC HOLIDAYS

The parks do get busier during the French Public Holidays – and there are lots of them! Days to avoid unless you like the crowds are:

- Jour de l'an (New Year's Day): 1st January
- Easter (date varies): March / April
- Lundi de Pâques: 12th April
- Fête du Travail (Labour Day): 1st May
- Fête de la Libération (Victory Day): 8th May
- Whitsun (Pentecôte): Last Monday in May
- Fête Nationale (Bastille Day): 14th July
- Assomption (Assumption Day): 15th August
- Toussaint (Halloween / All Saint's Day): 31st Oct – 1st November
- Le jour de Noël (Christmas Day): 25th December

Remember also that August is traditionally holiday month in France; kids who stay close to home may visit the parks.

When To Visit

Typically the parks are quieter when the weather isn't that great; you'll freeze your ears off but you will get on all of the rides without queuing! But you can't beat a sunny day, everything just looks shinier and even more amazing when the rays beam down. The best time to go really depends what you want to do and who you are with.

Avoid Bank holidays - the French hols are on the previous page. It's sooooo busy then!

What's On When...

Whenever you come to Disneyland® Resort Paris there will be lots to do, but there are some extra special events that happen around the same time every year. Check 🖳 www.knapsackguides.com for actual dates. Five smile events below are best (duh!).

Month	Events	Rating
January	New Year at Disneyland® Resort Paris is a very special occasion, with even more fireworks lighting up the sky and great parties in the Disneyland® hotels.	☺☺☺☺
Feb.	Chinese New Year goes with a bang!. Features a dancing dragon and spectacular fireworks celebrating all things eastern.	☺☺☺
March	17th St Patrick's Day Celebration - look out for shamrocks and leprechauns (cheeky little pixies!).	☺☺
July	Festival Latina - get down to a bit of salsa and samba with the Latino beat - yippee!	☺☺☺☺
Oct.	Frontierland turns into Halloweenland - highly recommended!!!	☺☺☺☺☺
Nov.	Bonfire Night, there will be many firework displays in and around Disneyland Resort Paris® commemorating Guy Fawkes' attempt to blow up Parliament in London.	☺☺☺☺
Dec.	The big Christmas Tree goes up and there are lights and decorations everywhere, especially down Main Street USA®.	☺☺☺☺☺

Keeping in Touch

Snail Mail
The Disneyland® Post Office is in Marne la Vallée Train Station. You can buy stamps in hotels or in the shops. Post boxes in France are bright yellow with a kind of horn on them (a musical horn not an animal one!).

E-mail
It is handy to have an e-mail account that you can access from anywhere. Popular choices are 'hotmail' or 'yahoo'. Whilst there are not any Internet cafés in the Disneyland® Parks, there are access points in the hotels, but watch out, these can be quite expensive.

INTERNET WARNING
Remember to be careful when you are using the internet, especially in chat rooms. NEVER give your name and address and NEVER meet anyone you make friends with unless you have the full approval of your parents and or guardian. This might sound dull but it is really important, just don't put yourself at risk.

Telephones
There are card and coin operated telephones in the parks and in the Disney® Village. France Télécom phone cards are sold at the Post Office and in shops.

Dosh
The money (currency), in France is the Euro (€). Each euro is made up of 100 cents (c). Notes are in €100, €50, €20, €10, €5 and €1 denominations. Coins are €2, €1, 50c, 20c, 10c, 5c, 2c and 1c.

If you want to know what your spending money is worth in euros you need to check the exchange rate. e.g. currently £1 is equal to €1.43, so £20 is €28.60.

Time to.....
The time in France is GMT +1 hours, one hour ahead of the UK. So 1000 in Paris is 0900 in London.

PHONE TIPS

If you are calling a telephone number in France from the UK you should dial the code to make an international call (00), then 33 for France and then miss the zero at the start of the no.

☎ Sea·Life Paris Val d'Europe Aquarium – (0)1 60 42 33 66.

EG, if you call the Sea·Life Aquarium from the UK you would dial:

00	international call code
33	UK code
1 60	Val d'Europe code
42 33 66	the rest of the telephone number

If you are calling a telephone number in the UK from France you should dial the code to make an international call (00), then 44 for the UK and then miss the first zero at the start of the number.

☎ Knapsack Beach Hut – 01273 737276

EG, if you call the Knapsack Beach Hut from France you would dial:

00	international call code
44	UK code
1273	Hove code
73 72 76	the rest of the telephone number

Phrasebook

One of the most exciting things about going to Disneyland® Resort Paris is the chance to try out your French. Most of the cast members do speak good English, but they will be dead impressed if you have a go at a bit of the old Français!

Essential Basics

English	French	Saying it
I don't understand	Je ne comprends pas	Je ne com-pron pa
Do you speak English?	Parlez-vous anglais?	Par-lay voo on-glay?
At what time?	á quelle heure?	a-kell-oor?
How much is it?	C'est combien?	say com-bee-en?
I would like...	Je voudrais...	Je voo-dray...
Where are the loos?	ou sont les toilettes?	oo son lay twa-let-es?

Even More Essential Basics

English	French	Saying it
yep!	oui	wwee (honestly!)
no	non	naun
please	s'il vous plait	see-voo play
thanks	merci	mer-see
hi !	salut!	sall-oo
goodbye	au revoir	oh rev-war
excuse me	excusez moi	excus-ai mwa
soz	pardon	par-dohn
How are you?	Ça va?	sa-va ?
I'm fine, thanks	Ça va bien, merci	sa-va be-an mer-see
ok	d'ac (d'accord)	dak

Fun Stuff!

English	French	Saying it
Bother !	zut !	zoot
a little brat	un sale gosse	un sal gos
be quiet	ferme la bouche	fer-may la boosh
Hands off my backpack!	Touche pas mon sac à dos!	Too-shay pa maw sac-a-dos!
There is a yellow rhinoceros in the bath	Il y a un rhinocéros jaune dans la baignoire	eel-ee-a un ree-nos-eros don la ban-war

Disney® Characters

Some of the Disney® Characters have different names in French – show your superior knowledge by using the French name. Also useful when you are getting autographs.

Chip n Dale	Tic & Tac	tic ett tac
Goofy	Dingo	ding-go
Winnie-the-Pooh	Winnie l'Ourson	winnee loor-son
Snow White	Blanche Neige	blon-sh nee-edge
Seven Dwarves	Sept Nains	set nines

Accidents and Emergencies

Hopefully you won't need to know this bit; but just in case. If you have an accident and need an emergency repair job done you can be taken to the First Aid point at the top of Main Street USA® in the Disneyland® Park and in the Front Lot in the Walt Disney Studios© Park.

They have fully trained nursing staff who will tend to your needs and sort you out.

MEDICAL EMERGENCY

In case of a real medical emergency or serious accident or if you need the Police or Fire Brigade you should telephone the emergency number below from any telephone and clearly ask for help - 'Aidez moi' (ay-day mwa).

Service :	☎ Tel:
Medical / Samu	☎ 15
Police / Gendarmerie	☎ 17
Fire / Pompier	☎ 18

Take a deep breath and tell the person on the end of the line your name, where you are and details about the problem, speak slowly as they may not speak very good English. Stay on the line until the person tells you to hang up. It is very important that you only do this in an emergency, if you cause a false alarm you might stop the emergency services going to a real accident and someone else might die. You will get into big trouble so be warned!

Special Needs

Getting the Info.

Disney® make a real effort to make sure the resorts can be enjoyed by absolutely anybody and absolutely everybody. 'The Special Services Guest Guide' and a 'Disabled Guests Guide' can be picked-up at City Hall as you enter the Disneyland® Park, at Studio Services in the Walt Disney Studios© Park or at hotel receptions. They tell you everything you need to know to make sure you have a ball (not brawl!).

TOP 5 FOR VISUALLY IMPAIRED

- Space Mountain, Discoveryland®
- Big Thunder Mountain, Frontierland®
- Indiana Jones™ and the Temple of Peril - Backwards, Adventureland®
- Rock 'n' Roller Coaster starring Aerosmith, Walt Disney Studios©
- Pirates of the Caribbean, Adventureland®

bathrooms with rails and high loos as well as handy wheelchair height spy holes.

When you arrive...

Go to the guest relations desk in City Hall in the Disneyland® Park with the relevant papers to prove your disability, they will

WHEEL-CHAIR TOP 5

- Honey I Shrunk The Audience, Discoveryland®
- Thunder Mesa River Boat, Frontierland®
- Studio Tram Tour, Walt Disney Studios©
- It's a Small World, Fantasyland®
- Flying Carpet Over Agrabah, Walt Disney Studios©

A Braille version is available for a small (returnable) deposit. For a sneak preview download it from: 🖥 www.disneyland-paris.com/uk.

Staying There

Over 100 rooms across all of the Disneyland® Paris hotels have been altered, with huge

TREATS!

- Exclusive areas at shows and parades (best views).
- Special access areas for some rides (although you can't skip the queue!).
- Discount on entrance passports and at some hotels (sometimes). For you and up to 3 others travelling with you.

then give you an easy access card that will grant you the special treats - most important! They will also be able to answer questions, give you advice or provide special help.

THE FACTS

Disney® History

WALT'S STORY

Once upon a time, in a land far, far away, well in 1901 in Chicago, America, a little boy was born, Walter Elias Disney. His parents weren't very rich and his dad's businesses kept failing so they moved around a lot, not much fun for little Walt.

But he grew up a bit of a cheeky chap, eager to do any job that came his way, from selling drinks on trains to painting camouflage on hats during World War One. After the war he went home to Kansas City (where Dorothy from the 'Wizard of Oz' came from) and started working in an advertising agency. He loved the movies that were getting really popular, so much so that he decided to pack his bags and try his luck in Hollywood.

Walt had been developing cartoon characters, but hadn't mastered the art of selling, then in 1928 it all came together with his famous creation, 'Mickey Mouse'. From this started the Disney empire that was to grow to cover cartoons, films and then theme parks - where people could live the Disney Dream.

Sadly, Walt only got to see Disneyland in California. During the planning of the Florida park Walt's bad cough got worse, a real cause for concern. Suddenly in 1966, just one week after his 65th birthday celebrations he keeled over and popped his clogs. Such a sad end to a real genius.

Willie or won't he?

Mickey Mouse was the star in Walt's cartoon 'Steamboat Willie', the first film ever to have sound in time to the pictures. It was all Walt's work, even Mickey's squeaks, sighs and whistles were from the man himself. It was very successful and allowed Walt, with his brother Roy, to create the fantastic Disney® Empire.

Bringing it to Life

Walt wanted to bring his creations to life by developing a Theme Park where both adults and children could fully experience the Disney magic for themselves. In was in 1955 that his dream came true. The first Disneyland Park® and the world's first ever theme park opened in California, a brilliant success. Walt was inspired, wanting to build them all over the world.

HIDDEN MICKEYS...

Some say there are hidden Mickeys all over the Disneyland® Parks. They started out as a joke amongst Disney Imagineers. who'd add a Mickey Mouse head and ears silhouette to places, just to see if anyone noticed. Now finding hidden Mickeys is a secret past-time for avid Disney fans! See if you spot any in Disneyland® , tell us if you do!

Florida Fantasy

Florida was to site the next park. However before construction work could start Walt died.

It was left to the rest of the Disney family to make Walt's Florida fantasy a reality. In 1971, five years after his death, the huge and amazing Walt Disney World Resort opened in Orlando, hurrah!

Going Global

Tokyo was the next venue, the first outside America. Opened in 1983 it has been visited by more than 260 million people so far.

Europe was always part of Walt's dream. But where should it be built? Finally France was chosen 'cos there was a massive bit of free land just outside Paris, very handy for lots of people to visit.

Rapid Redevelopment

Work started in 1987. It took only four years for the first bits of work to be completed; slowly the fairytale theme park began to come alive. The pink turrets of Sleeping Beauty's castle peeped over the fence, the roller coaster rides stood ready to thrill and Mickey Mouse fever began to sweep across the surrounding area. Finally the doors to the Magic Kingdom opened on the 12th April 1992.

HIGH RISE?

Sleeping Beauty's castle is 43m high, less than half the size of Big Ben! It looks higher as the clever Disney® people have designed it to trick our eyes. The illusion is called 'forced perspective'.

Next Please!
It didn't stop there.... There has been lots of development since the park opened to make it an even better experience. The opening of the Walt Disney Studios© Park on the 16th March 2002 was a great example of this, allowing visitors to find out a bit more about the magic of Disney.

Disneyland Resort Paris® Facts
The Disneyland Resort Paris® is about 20 miles south east of Paris, in an area called 'Marne la Vallée'. It covers 1,943 hectares – that is really enormous, about 1/5 of the size of Paris itself! Less than half of the land (900 hectares to be precise) has been developed, still plenty of room for it to grow and get even better!

Disney® Characters

The magic of Disney® is brought to life through the amazing Disney® characters. From the cheeky chap Mickey Mouse to more recent characters like Mulan and Nemo, you can't help liking them. Some other characters have

also been 'disneyfied' giving them even wider appeal, favourites like Winnie the Pooh and Peter Pan. Meeting the characters is one of the best things about going to the Parks, getting their autographs is even better, take your autograph book.

A favourite are the Disney® Princesses who cuddle up to their Prince Charmings. From Sleeping Beauty to Snow White, Cinderella to Ariel, Mulan, Belle and Jasmine, you can see them all and even have breakfast with them. They are truly beautiful, but probably more of a girl thing than a boy thing.

Why do Tigger's hands smell? Because he's been playing with Pooh all day!

Think of a word which is singular, but when you add an "s" it becomes plural, and when you add another "s" it becomes singular again...
(Answer: Prince)

Disney® People

An unbelievable 12,500 people work at Disneyland® Paris! Called 'Cast Members', they come from all over the world - from at least 50 different countries.

All Cast Members go to the Disney University to learn what is allowed and what isn't, they are very strict you know! If they pass they are awarded a Mousters Degree or a Ducktorate Degree.

Some of the most important people that work in the Parks are the 'Imagineers'. These amazing people invent and create the rides and attractions, thinking about every-

Try this tongue twister 'Can you imagine an imaginary menagerie manager imagining managing an imaginary menagerie?'

THINGS YOU LEARN AT THE DISNEY UNIVERSITY

- Never cross your arms or point, indicate with the whole hand.
- You can lean whilst you are working, but you must not be seen slouching or sitting down!
- Tattoos, red nail polish & facial hair are decorations of the devil.
- Disney Lingo – visitors are guests, workers are cast members, uniforms are costumes, when you are visible to 'guests' you are on stage, if you are not visible you are backstage.
- You must smile (and not just with your mouth) and be happy at ALL times.

Sounds like hard work!

thing in minute detail. When you look around the park check out how much effort has been made to make things just perfect, from the boots in the tent on the way through to Indiana Jones™ Temple of Peril to the little pigs in the Pirates of the Caribbean.

Disneyland® Resort Paris Visitors

Since it opened more than 110 million people have passed through the Magic Kingdom gates in Paris. It

is the number one tourist destination in Europe, with currently 13.1 million people enjoying the trip every year. Amazing! Of these 18% of guests (2.3 million) come from the UK and most stay for 3 nights / 4 days. Twice as many people visit Disneyland Resort Paris® compared to the Eiffel Tower, and nearly 5 times as many people visit than the number going to Alton Towers.

In the summer about 50-60 thousand people visit every day, they stop letting people in when 62 thousand people are inside!

HANGING OUT -
THE DISNEYLAND® PARK...

Disneyland Park®

Main Street USA© awaits as you go through the gates of the Disneyland Park®. The rest of the lands are all around you, with the Central Plaza at the core.

LAND FACTS

● **Main Street USA©**

Where you arrive as you walk through the park gates. Like a tiny town in America in the early 1900's, so cute! You can't help smiling as you make your way past the cheery railway station and sweet shops. The street leads up to the Central Plaza where the amazing parades are held every day.

● **Frontierland©**

You'll think you are in the Wild West when you enter here. Home of Big Thunder Mountain and the Phantom Manor. If you are a sure shot get a bit of practise in at the Shootin' Gallery or if you fancy a tranquil river ride go on the Paddle Steamer.

● **Adventureland©**

From the oriental bazaar of Aladdin's Palace you enter the tropical land of danger and hidden treasures. See the mysterious lagoon, explore the sinister caves (you're certain to get lost) or scare the pants of the grown ups by jumping on the wobbly rope bridge, and that's before you even been on the rides. Our favourite!

● **Fantasyland©**

Creep past the dragon guarding 'Sleeping Beauty's Castle' (he's right underneath) into toddler paradise! There are some fun things in here, but it really caters mainly for the little ones.

● **Discoveryland©**

It's back to the future in Discoveryland. There is a lot to experience's here with all sorts of special effects and technological wizardry to wow your socks off. Don't miss 'Honey I Shrunk The Audience', a real laugh with a few surprising twists.

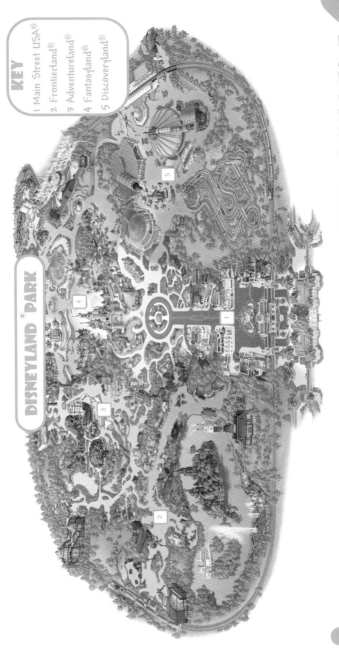

KEY

1. Main Street USA®
2. Frontierland®
3. Adventureland®
4. Fantasyland®
5. Discoveryland®

DISNEYLAND® PARK

Hanging Out - On The Rides

Let's be honest, this is the bit you're here for and you are so going to love it! There are rides to suit everyone from the slow pretty ones, to the hang on to your pants and stomach ones.

As well as telling you about the rides, we have also used icons, so you can see at a glance what a ride is like - see the key at the bottom of the page. They are:

- ♁ Height restriction
- 🏎 Thrilling
- ☠ Spooky
- 🎭 Theatrical
- ◀🔊 Noisy
- 🐎 Gentle
- ♿ Wheelchair access
- 🕐 Set times

Also look out for the overall rating where a ride is given a mark out of five thumbs ups (👍)

👍👍👍👍👍	Unforgettable, unbelievable, unmissable
👍👍👍👍	Wicked, one to have on the 'must do' list
👍👍👍	Pretty good
👍👍	OK, but won't set the world alight
👍	Pretty rubbish
👎	Totally rubbish, only go to laugh at it!

Remember this is just our opinion, you might not agree. If you don't then drop us a line at
🖥www.knapsackguides.com. Also, most of the
👍👍👍👍👍 rides will rides be really popular so make sure you go there first or use a Fastpass if you can.

Frontierland©
Big Thunder Mountain

📷 Frontierland©
♁ 1.02m
ⓘ 🏎 ◀🔊 Fastpass
Rating: 👍👍👍👍

Get ready to go wild in the Wild West. Set in a rocky, mountainous desert in America, it is really well done, you can just imag-

TOP 5
THRILLING
RIDES

- Space Mountain, Discoveryland©
- Rock 'N' Roller Coaster, Walt Disney Studios©
- Indiana Jones™ & the Temple of Peril: Backwards!, Adventureland©
- Big Thunder Mountain, Frontierland©
- Star Tours, Discoveryland©

...ine you are a miner off to work when things go terribly wrong...

At peak times this ride can get busy as the turnaround is not that fast so a good place to use the Fastpass. The queuing system is well designed but a bit deceptive, just as you think you are almost there you find out you still have a way to go.

The train starts off slowly and then hurtles into the mine workings, winding its way through bats and caves. If you survive that it's onto a flooding river with seemingly no more track, watch out for the water.

A great ride, quite jerky but fun and long enough that you feel the queuing was worth it. Definitely one not to miss.

Adventureland©
Indiana Jones™ and the Temple of Peril: Backwards!

Adventureland©
⋂ 1.40m
ⓘ ✍ ◄» Fastpass
Rating: ♦♦♦♦♦

It was a thriller when it went forwards, now it is a super thriller going backwards. It is even better than normal roller coasters as you just can't see what is going to happen next, the deep plunges and the loop the loops are brilliant. The archaeological dig setting has also been done really well, making the queue much more interesting than usual.

⋂ Height restriction   ✍ Thrilling   ⚝ Spooky   ⁛ Theatrical
◄» Noisy   ⁜ Gentle   ♿ Wheelchair access   ⊙ Set times

Pirates of the Caribbean

📷 Adventureland©

ⓘ 🏊 ✂ 👤
Rating: ♦♦♦♦

Whilst this is gentle it is quite magical, worth going on a couple of times to make sure you catch it all. The characters that live in the secret dingy depths of the Caribbean underworld sing and jeer as you float past on your boat, passing skeletons and treasures, skulduggery and treachery. There are a couple of fun splashes too as you drop into the caverns and you also float past the diners in the 'Blue Lagoon' restaurant. Excellent!

Fantasyland©

There are loads of rides here, but most are really for little kids (under 8's). Whilst they are cute and sweet they won't get your heart thumping. If you are a fairy fancier then they will really be your thing, if you are a hard core adrenalin junkie they really are best missed. Here are the better rides:

> What do you call an elephant that can't do maths?
> Dumbo!

Blanche-Neige Et Les Sept Nains

📷 Fantasyland©

ⓘ 👤 ✂
Rating: ♦♦

Enjoy the story of Snow White and the Seven Dwarves (in French) as you travel on board a diamond mining cart travelling through dark mines. The best bit is the wicked queen and apple scene, mildly spooky and a little entertaining.

Peter Pan's Flight

📷 Fantasyland©

ⓘ 👤 ✂ Fastpass
Rating: ♦♦♦

Get here early as it is a slow loader, very, very popular and the queues get huge even in the quietest times! It's another boat ride, this time flying in a pirate boat over the sights of night time London to Neverland.   This is what Fantasyland© is all about.

Mad Hatter's Tea Cups

Fantasyland©

ⓘ 🌀

Rating: ◔◔◔

If you are a fairground 'Waltzers' fan then you'll like this one. Sit right in a tea cup spin and spin and spin, exciting but not good straight after lunch!   You can control the speed – the faster the better.

'It's a small world'

Fantasyland©

ⓘ ❦ ♿

Rating: ❧ or ◔◔◔

You'll either love it or hate it!   Hop into your canal boat for your gentle globe trotting trip passing 280 little dolls dressed up in the national costumes of countries throughout the world.   The little Scottish lassie is there in her kilt, the Hawaiian chick in her grass skirt and the cute little Eskimo fishing for dinner; all to the mind numbing 'it's a small world' theme tune. One to take your great granny on, she'll love it!

Discoveryland©
Autopia

Discoveryland©

ⓝ 1.32m for drivers

ⓘ ❦

Rating: ◔◔

This ride is good, but could be a bit of a let down for some because you don't really get to drive freely, you are guided along a track. Probably more suited for littler kids (so long as they meet the height restrictions). It also gets soooooo busy so get there early or go during the parade times.

ⓝ Height restriction 🌀 Thrilling ☙ Spooky ⸙ Theatrical
⸎ Noisy ❦ Gentle ♿ Wheelchair access ⊙ Set times

Space Mountain

Discoveryland©
1.32m
Fastpass
Rating: ♦♦♦♦♦

One of the best and most exciting rides in the park. Hold on tight 'cos you shoot around the course so quickly with bends and plunges galore right from the moment you  are blasted to the moon – you need to scream to breathe! Travelling 1km in 3 minutes you nearly hit a meteorite and flash by the stars, unable to anticipate what comes next as it is all in the dark. The music and lights add to the atmosphere – NOT TO BE MISSED!

Star Tours

Discoveryland©
Fastpass
Rating: ♦♦♦♦

A must for all Star Wars™ fans – and worth a go for those who hate the film too! You queue in the space station attended by know-all droids R-2D2 and C-P30 as you wait to board your Star Speeder spacecraft.

Try to get a seat at the front for the most fearsome fun. Be prepared for an intrepid jerky, bumpy ride into the unknown. Don't forget the Star Course Video Game at the end, it is also fantastic (height restriction of 1.02m).

Orbitron®

⊡ Discoveryland©
ⓘ 🚹
Rating: 👀

Another fun and popular ride with the space theme. You climb into your space ship and spin around and up and down. Controls are in the front for those who like to be in charge.

Hanging Out - In Scary Places

What is it about scary places that make them that bit more exciting? Who knows... but don't you just love them!

Frontierland© is the home of fear. Most of the year this is due to the presence of the fantastic Phantom Manor, but it is especially so in October when the place undergoes a transformation and becomes Halloweenland©. It is spooktastically cool.

Phantom Manor

⊡ Frontierland©
ⓘ 🚹♪
Rating: 👀👀

The neglected old Victorian manor house is set in the midst of the mysterious Thunder Mesa and was home to the beautiful maiden Melanie Ravenswood, daughter of one of the early settlers.

Tragically, on the very day she was going to get married, an evil and deranged phantom appeared and savagely killed her husband-to-be, hanging him, blood dripping, from the ceiling.

DID YOU KNOW?

The plaque reading 'Non Omnis Moriar' on the gate to the manor means 'I will not completely die'. A message from Melanie...

♠ Height restriction   🚹 Thrilling   🎭 Spooky   Theatrical
♪ Noisy   Gentle   ♿ Wheelchair access   Set times

Legend has it that Melanie was so heart broken that she never took her wedding dress off and has since been joined by 998 other ghosts to haunt the spooky rooms.

When you enter the manic mansion you are ushered into a round room and after an announcement (in French) welcoming you, the room starts to stretch and you plunge deep into the house (with a few surprises on the way!). You then stroll through the haunted house and climb into one of the 130 "doom buggies" to begin the toe curling tour. Good fun with ace audio-animatronic effects and not really that scary unless you are a pathetic, puny wimp or a little kid.

PHANTOM FACTS

- The ride opened on April 12th, 1992.
- The ride lasts about 5½ minutes plus a 2-minute pre-show presentation.
- There are 130 "Doombuggies" on 240 meters of track, with 6 back-up cars.
- 92 Audio-Animatronics are used along with 58 individual special effects.
- 54 animated props add atmosphere along with more than 400 special show props.

Boot Hill Cemetery

Frontierland©
ⓘ ⚥
Rating: ♦♦♦

A great way to finish off your trip around the Phantom Manor is to creep around the shadowy Boot Hill Cemetery. Watch out when you are near the huge four poster grave, it sounds like there must be someone in there...maybe they'll get you - aaaaagh!!!

Some of the gravestones are funny and worth a giggle, see if you can find 'Peg Leg McBrogue, the river rogue, who walked the plank and sank'! Others are inscribed with the names of some Imagineers who worked on the creation of the manor.

Halloweenland©

As Summer comes to an end and Winter beckons strange things start to happen in the Disneyland® Park. Main Street USA© turns into Spooky Street, sinister but safe in comparison to the seriously scary Frontierland© that is Halloweenland©. Are you brave enough to visit the kingdom of terror?

Disney® know how to create mysterious, manic mayhem (mind the massive wispy web at the entrance), spooky special effects and spine-chilling shows to celebrate Halloween. All kinds of extra activities also take place – fantastic face paints, cosy coffins to take a nap in, horribly happening Halloween parties and not forgetting the amazing Halloween Parade.

TOP SPOTTING SPOTS

The best places for watching the Halloween Parade are:

- In front of the queuing area of 'It's A Small World'.
- From the balcony on top of the director's booth behind the seats of the Castle Stage.
- From the pavilion at Town Square .
- From the Railroad's Main Street Station (fav. photo spot).

Why did the boy carry a clock and a bird on Halloween?
It was for "tick or tweet"!

Hanging Out - At The Shows

This section covers the visual spectacles in the Parks, the theatrical shows and the places where you wander about looking around and exploring. The last bit might sound boring but it isn't honest! You can't deny

Height restriction | Thrilling | Spooky | Theatrical
Noisy | Gentle | Wheelchair access | Set times

it, Disney® knows how to put on a good show, and they certainly do this at Disneyland Resort Paris®! Some also come with a few surprises, but we won't tell the secrets, we don't want to spoil anything do we?

Chaparral Theatre

▣ Frontierland©

ⓘ ✎ ♿ ⏲ (Lasts 25 mins)
Rating: ◊◊◊◊

The rating here depends on the show, but they do tend to be pretty spectacular! With dancing, music and lots of Disney® magic you will be captivated by the on stage antics, all in a groovy natural setting. The Tarzan show is especially sensational, the monkeys will totally wow, they jump so high with fantastic acrobatics. Some of the shows even give you a chance to get up on stage yourself, maybe a little bit embarrassing but you never know, could be your route to stardom!

Fantasy Festival Stage

▣ Fantasyland©

ⓘ ✎ ♿ ⏲ (Timing Varies - ask at City Hall)
Rating: ◊◊◊ / ◊◊

This may be the smallest of all of the Disneyland® theatres, but it does often feature the Big Five. When these guys are going to perform get there early, you need to be there at least 30 minutes in advance. At other times you get visiting acts; singers, dancers, bands and the like doing a turn under the 'Magic Music Days' banner. Sometimes quite entertaining but not worth queuing for! This is one of the venues for the Disney® Christmas celebrations.

BIG FIVE?

Mickey, Minnie, Donald Duck, Goofy and Pluto

Le Théâtre du Château

◖ Fantasyland©

ⓘ 🍴 ♿ ⏱ (Lasts 25 mins)
Rating: 🍦

This is an open air theatre looking on to the magical Sleeping Beauty's castle, a really amazing spectacle on a sunny day but not that fun when it's pouring with rain! Usually they only have shows here during the summer, no big surprise.

To be honest the shows are very cute but a little bit babyish, this is Fantasyland® after all. Recent stars have been Winnie the Pooh, Tigger, Piglet and Rabbit in a musical comedy, it has its own charm but not when there are exciting rides to go on!

> What do Winnie-the-Pooh and Coco the Clown have in common?
> The same middle name!

Honey I Shrunk The Audience

◖ Discoveryland©

ⓘ 🍴 ♿
Rating: 🍦🍦🍦🍦

Prepare to be put down to size at this show! Entering the -holding area at the start you are told all about the Imagination Institute and their world famous inventor, Wayne Szalinski in a funny little film. After putting on your trendy, yellow safety goggles (they are really 3D glasses), you go through to the special award ceremony for Mr Szalinski. But watch out, things don't go quite according to plan when he tries to demonstrate his revolutionary shrinking and enlargening machine. It's really funny with fab special effects and lots of surprises; hope you're not scared of mice...

> What do you get if cross a mouse with a bottle of shampoo?
> Bubble and squeak!!

♬ Height restriction	⚡ Thrilling	👻 Spooky	🎭 Theatrical
🔊 Noisy	🌿 Gentle	♿ Wheelchair access	⏱ Set times

Le Visionarium (The Visionarium)

Discoveryland©

① ⏱ ♿ ⏲ (Lasts 20 mins)
Rating: 👀👀

You need eyes in the back of your head, and the front of your head and at the sides of your head to really appreciate the 360° film here! 'Nine eye' a funky futuristic robot takes you back in time to meet Jules Verne, the bloke who wrote 'Around the World In 80 Days'. The story is much better than the usual scenery and landscape ones you usually get in these kinds of places, with a few groovy special effects.   Probably lasts a little to long at 20 minutes

Les Mystères du Nautilus (The Mysteries of Nautilus)

Discoveryland©

① ⏱ ♿
Rating: 👀👀👀

Next to Space Mountain ride it's worth investigating Captain Nemo's submarine from '20,000 Leagues under the Sea' another book by Jules Verne. You

JULES RULES

Jules Verne was a bit of a dude, together with HG Wells he started the whole Science Fiction thing. Just think if it hadn't been for him there might not have been any Star Wars, Star Trek or Matrix.

wander around yourself so you are free to explore all of the nooks and crannies, the detail is quite amazing. It could be a bit more exciting, the squid attack isn't that scary but worth a visit anyway.

Videopolis

Discoveryland©

① ⏱ ♿⏲ (Lasts 25 mins)
Rating: 👀👀

This theatre is inside the fancy Café Hyperion and is where the extravagant shows are held a number of times every day, get there half and hour in advance if you want the best view. The shows are pretty cool, starring Mickey and his mates. They usually last about half an hour and are pure Disney® , maybe a little bit young for you, more for the under 8's. You can also eat here, self service burgers and chicken nuggets.

Who has huge antlers, a high voice and wears white gloves?
Mickey Moose!

Hanging Out - At The Parades

Everyday Extravaganzas

Disney® are famous for their Parades and they deserve to be as they are pretty awesome!

Every day there is at least one amazing float procession making its way past Fantasyland© and down through Main Street USA©. You must go to the daily parade (c. 4pm) at least once during your visit; it is true

PARADE TOP TIPS

- The Band Stand at the Town Square is a good spot to watch.
- Watch the parade come down towards you, then nip up through the arcades to get to Central Plaza to watch the Parade on its return trip.

that the rides get a lot quieter at this time but the parades are too good to miss. Disney® at its best.

◯ Height restriction   📷 Thrilling   👻 Spooky   Theatrical
🔊 Noisy   Gentle   ♿ Wheelchair access   Set times

Themed Dreams

The themes of the parades change regularly, sometimes according to the season and other times just to inject a bit of variety for the crowds and for the cast members. They always feature the Big Five

WATCHING AT WALT'S

For a special treat, or in the winter when it is very cold, you can have dinner at Walt's on Main Street USA© and watch the parades from the window seats. The seats can't be guaranteed but if you can get one it is really amazing.

along with the famous characters from the top Disney® films and lots of beautiful dancers.

Lights Up

The evening parades are even more spectacular if that is possible. Millions of little lights twinkle in the darkness to make the magic feel even stronger. There is

also something special about watching it all with a dark backdrop, it makes it all a bit more exciting. Finally you just can't beat the scenery, especially Sleeping Beauty's Castle as it towers over the whole spectacle.

Spectacular Spectaculars

If you plan to visit in October then make sure you go to the Halloween parade. It's spooks galore as all things creepy slip their way down through Halloweenland© (Frontierland© in disguise!) to ghastly, ghostly tunes. Totally gruesome, totally great!

The Christmas parade is especially incredible; with Mickey and Minnie in cute Christmas costumes it certainly fills you with festive spirit. You'll definitely be singing jingle bells all the way! Christmas in Disneyland Resort® Paris isn't just in December; it lasts from mid November until mid January. It's just a pity that it is usually absolutely freezing.

Did you hear about Dracula's Christmas party? It was a scream!

⋂ Height restriction   ⚡ Thrilling   🕯 Spooky   Theatrical
↻ Noisy   Gentle ♿ Wheelchair access Set times

Walt Disney Studios© Park.

Currently this is quite a bit smaller than the Disneyland® Park but it is bound to grow and get even better. It is also different in terms of look and atmosphere; less fairy dust and more technical wizardry. It is divided into four easy to get around areas, we have covered them clockwise from the Front Lot as you enter the park.

ACCESS ALL AREAS

● Front Lot

Access all areas through the Front Lot, an under cover studio area housing a boutique boulevard and mega eating area. A handy place to go if it's raining. Real films are made here, a chance to be a film star maybe? Have a dig around behind the scenes, plenty to explore.

● Production Courtyard

Go straight to the 'Studio Tram Tour®', <u>the</u> place to start. You really get to see behind the scenes, but be careful, things can go wrong. The 'Television Production Tour' also starts here (go on this just for the design-your-own-roller coaster ride – thrill-tastic), right next door to the nostalgic (if a bit boring) 'Cinémagique' show.

● Backlot

Three action packed attractions feature here, the unmissable 'Rock 'n' Roller Coaster Starring Aerosmith', the 'Moteurs...Action!' Stunt Show Spectacular and the 'Armageddon' special effects show. The Rock 'n' Roller Coaster is one of the best in the whole of the resort, it is <u>so</u> fast, your stomach really does end up in your throat. Terrrrrrific!

● Animation Courtyard

If 'toons are your thing then you'll love it here. The 'Art of Disney Animation®' shows you how cartoons are made whilst 'Animagique®' is an inspirational blend of animation and imagination. Finally you can catch a ride in a magic carpet over Agrabah® and the rest of the park.

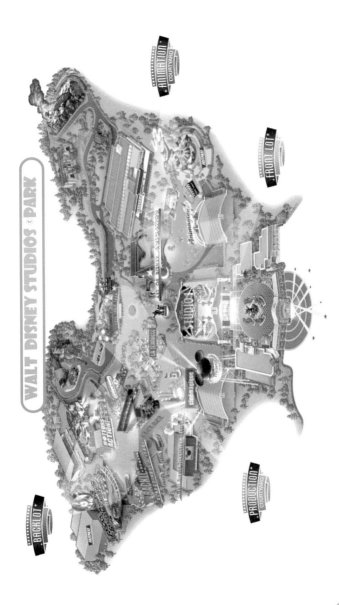

WALT DISNEY STUDIOS PARK

Hanging Out - On The Rides

Studio Tram Tour®: Behind The Magic
Production Courtyard
ⓘ 🔖
Rating: ♦♦♦♦

This is a great introduction to the wonders of Disney®. Make sure you are in the right part of the Tram to hear the English commentary - it's not that

good in Spanish! Passing by real props from movies (Pearl Harbour, 101 Dalmatians) you find out lots of insider secrets before you reach the set of 'Catastrophe Canyon'. It is a little alarming here; people don't really seem to know what they are doing. Do be careful, it can get a bit messy. The

tour then moves on behind more scenes, past some groovy genuine movie cars to the set of the 2002 film 'Reign of Fire', set in London. It is amazingly life like – and a bit spooky. Don't miss!

Rock 'n' Roller Coaster Starring Aerosmith
Backlot
ⓘ 🔖 ◀» 🔖 Fastpass
Rating: ♦♦♦♦♦

One of the best, if not THE best ride in Disneyland Resort Paris®. You queue amongst masses of rock and roll memorabilia to board the sharpest shuttle ever. Anticipation reaches supersonic heights as the countdown flashes in front

DID YOU KNOW?

The Rock 'n' Roller Coaster blasts off doing 0-60mph in 2.8 seconds – faster than most sports cars. Terrific!

of you, and before you have a chance to catch your

breath you are off – feel the g's. Truly awesome!!! The thrill factor continues as you loop and twist with the booming sound of Aerosmith blasting from the superb sound system fitted in each car with light effects flashing in front of you. You'll just have to do it again... and again...

What kind of pet did Aladdin have?
A flying car-pet!

Flying Carpet Over Agrabah®
Animation Courtyard
ⓘ 🎫 Fastpass
Rating: 🌢🌢🌢

Keep a hold on your carpet and your stomach as you fly around the magic lamp in your four man magic rug. It's basically the same ride as the Orbitron / Dumbo in the other park, except front riders control the up and down and back seat riders the twist and turn. Gets busy, Fastpass it or arrive early.

Hanging Out - At The Shows

Cinémagique
Production Courtyard
ⓘ 🐌 ♿ 🕐 (Lasts 30 mins)
Rating: 🌢🌢🌢

If you like a good film then put this on your must visit list. When you've been on a few rides and you need a bit of a rest then sit back, relax and enjoy a funny, bizarre and very clever little film. Mind out if you sit near the front, especially if there is a strange guy sitting next to you... and remember to turn off your mobile 'phone, could be a little embarrassing otherwise... Maybe a bit grown up for littlies, but great for movie moguls. Check out the funny special effects, when you least expect them.

ⴖ Height restriction 🎫 Thrilling ❊ Spooky Theatrical
♪ Noisy Gentle ♿ Wheelchair access Set times

Moteurs...Action! Stunt Show Spectacular®

▸ Backlot
① ✔ ◁ʾ ♿ ⏰ (Lasts 45 mins)
Rating: ♦♦♦♦♦

Stunt Shows are coo-el, and this one won't disappoint. If you like car chases, motorbike wheelies or a good shoot out you'll be impressed and a bit wowed! Watch the high risk action unfold in front of you, and then watch it all over again on the screen so that you can see how the stunt works; it's clever stuff. You feel like you are right in the middle of the action and you

can even <u>be</u> part of the action. Members of the audience get to be part of the film, how groovy is that? Get there at least 30 minutes before the start to get one of the best seats near the front.

Armageddon

▸ Backlot
① ✔ ◁ʾ ♿ ⏰
Rating: ♦♦

One of the biggest disappointments. It's not bad, it's just that you expect it to be realllllllly good and it's just OK. The set up is a little confusing, but basically you are going on to the set for the next Armageddon film as an 'extra'. That takes about 10 minutes to say in a confusing mix of French with a bit of jokey English thrown in. After shuffling into the

> Knock, Knock
> Who's there?
> Armageddon
> Armageddon, who?
> Armageddon outa here!

space craft the 'adventure' begins. The place fills with smoke whilst rattles, bangs and hisses echo around as a meteor shower descends on the craft and the special effects begin. Stand in the middle for the biggest impact, but don't build up your expectations.

Animagique®

📷 Animation Courtyard
① 📷 ♪ ⑤ ⏱ (Lasts 25 mins)
Rating: 💧💧💧

With loads of special effects to entertain. Get right to the front (in the first 12 rows) to be in the middle of things – you'll find out what we mean. Bringing together expertise from across the globe; a special black light technique from the Czech Republic alongside massive, Japanese fluorescent puppets, all set loose by the dappy Donald Duck. Also stars Mickey, Dumbo, Pinocchio and stars of the Jungle Book and the Lion King, an animation extravaganza.

Hanging Out - At The Parades

Walt Disney Studios© is home to the Disney® Cinema Parade. You'll know when it is about to begin when the razzmatazz music pipes around the park and Goofy starts zipping around the park in his nippy go cart; it's a busy life when you are film director you know...

Stars in Your Eyes

The Oscar winners roll past in their looooong limousines, fancy a ride in one of those? Well you might get a chance one day, after you have appeared in Goofy's film. 'Cos you not only get to watch this parade, you also get to be a part of it. The cameras capture the

captivated crowd and you can take part – minding the 101 Dalmatians or directing the soldiers from Toy

○ Height restriction   ☑ Thrilling   ⚬ Spooky   Theatrical
◁⟩ Noisy   Gentle   ⚭ Wheelchair access   Set times

Story, great fun! A film of your antics will roll live on the last float.

The floats here are a little smaller than in the Disneyland Park® but they are a bit more action oriented, as much happens around the float as happens actually on the thing. Not to be missed!

Did you hear about the toy soldier that was in the army since he was a baby? He was in the infantry!

Hanging Out - Behind the Scenes

Want to find out how the Disney® magic is made? Then don't miss out the Television Production Tour or the Art of Disney Animation®.

Television Production Tour
◪ Production Courtyard
① ☜ ♿ (🎟 optional at end)
Rating: ♨♨♨ / ♨♨♨♨ (Roller Coaster)
Sneak behind the scene of the TV Studios where the Disney® TV Programmes are really made, you can even go right into the studios. Fascinating banks of screens and buttons and switches await you, pity you can't touch. The optional virtual rollercoaster ride at the end is a must - try level 4 if you're hard enough!

Art of Disney Animation®
◪ Animation Courtyard
① ☜ ♿⏱
Rating: ♨♨♨
This starts off a bit boring but then gets better and better.   Part exhibition (the dull bit), part film, part live presentation and then interactive, it gives a varied introduction to cartooning.   The animation stations at the end are totally brill, especially if you are good at drawing. You can create your own character - Disney® look out!

Hanging Out - With The Characters

The characters are what make Disney®, Disney®, you can't help get excited when you see them. If you don't then you are just a miserable grump – so there!

MEETING PLACES

Disneyland® Park

- Casey's Corner — Main Street USA©
- Storybook Store, Town Square — Main Street USA©
- Central Plaza — Main Street USA©
- Royal Castle Stage — Fantasyland©

Walt Disney Studios© Park

- Flying Carpets Over Agrabah® — Animation Courtyard
- Television Studios — Production Courtyard
- Ciné Folies - Disney Studio — Front Lot

In the Parks

The best places to get up close and personal are at the special 'Meet 'n' Greet' sessions. The allocated meeting places are clearly identified on the free park maps by a big Mickey's hand with details of the times.

CHARACTER ANTICS

- Get their autograph (with a thick pen - easier to hold)
- Have your photo taken
- Give them a huge cuddle
- Ask 'Is it hot in there?'
- Jump into other people's photographs pulling a funny face!

If you get to the Disneyland® Park nice and early you can catch Mickey and his mates at the 'Magical Main Street Welcome' in the first half hour of the park opening. They hang out on the platform outside the Liberty Arcade, in the Central Plaza area and at the Théâtre du Château to the right of the castle entrance.

TOP SECRET SIGHTINGS

- Grab the characters as they enter and leave the parks.
- In Disneyland® Park they use the gate next to 'It's A Small World' or the gate next to 'Bixby Brothers Shop'.
- At Walt Disney Studios© Park they take the gates by Studio 1 or the gate by 'Animagique®'.
- The Disneyland® Hotel is a great place as loads of guests are boring grown ups not that bothered about the characters.

At Hotels

The Characters hang out at the Disney® Hotel lobbies at set times during the day. Morning is a good time to catch them, take your camera and auto-graph book to breakfast to get in there first. This is one of the great benefits of staying at the Disney® resort hotels.

Eating With The Characters

☎ (0)1 60 45 60 45 for reservations

Booking a table for one of the character meals is a sure fire way to meet your favourite Disney® friend. Book in advance; these places get real-llllllly busy. 'Café Mickey' is popular 'cos it serves character meals through the whole day.

Hanging Out - Nosh!

Can you believe it - up to 150,000 meals are served every day at Disneyland® Resort Paris in the busy times, astounding!

TOP 5 PLACES FOR CHARACTER MEALS

- Walt's Restaurant, Main St USA© - breakfast
- Manhattan Restaurant, Disney's Hotel New York® - breakfast
- The Lucky Nugget Saloon, Frontierland© - lunch
- Café Mickey, Disney® Village - breakfast, lunch and dinner
- Inventions Restaurant, Disneyland® Hotel - breakfast and dinner

There is a huge variety of places to eat, from your standard chicken nuggets and burger specials to your posh napkin and fancy cutlery joints. Remember you are not allowed to

bring your own food into the Parks so you do have to either eat your picnic outside in the special picnic area; eat in one of the Disney® places or, at a stretch, drive to the Val d'Europe shopping centre. In the summer the last option isn't necessarily a bad one.

Most of the cafés and restaurants have special deals, like kid's menus and fixed price three course 'packages'. Some of these are a good deal, for example in the 'Fuente del Oro' you can have Chicken Nuggets and Chips, an Ice Cream and a Coke for just €5, or for a special treat in the 'Blue Lagoon' Restaurant you can have the 'Cabin Boy's Menu' of Grilled Swordfish Steak with Lemon Potatoes and a Volcano Dessert for €10. These menus are only available for 3-11 year olds.

Waiter, there is no chicken in these chicken nuggets! So what? You don't get dog in a dog biscuit, do you?

Bringing Your Own Picnic
Special Picnic Area
Rating: ♦♦♦

The big advantage of this is that you get to eat the food that you like, the disadvantage is that sandwiches go soggy by lunchtime!

You can either leave your picnic in your car (if you have one at the Park) or drop your bag off at the Left Luggage offices. There is one in each park: outside the Disneyland® Park, by the 'Guest Relations Window' and next to Studio Services at the entrance to the Walt Disney Studios© Park.

There is a special picnic area between the Visitors Car park and the Parks entrance and some picnic tables near the Disneyland® Hotel. You can buy delicious picnic food at the Auchan Hypermarket at Val d'Europe about 5 minutes drive away from the parks.

Snack Attack

When you feel a bit peckish or fancy a little treat then there is plenty to tempt your taste buds. Chomp a chewy choccie brownie, slurp a slippy, sloppy cornet or crunch a crispy, crumbly cookie – delish! Many of these places are generally only open during the summer and at weekends.

SNACK STOPS

- Cookie Kitchen / Cable Car Bake Shop, Main Street U.S.A.©
- The Coffee Grinder, Main Street, U.S.A.©
- The Gibson Girl Ice Cream Parlour, Main Street U.S.A.©
- The Ice Cream Company, Main Street U.S.A.©
- Café de la Brousse, Adventureland©
- Captain Hook's Galley, Adventureland©
- Fantasia Gelat, Fantasyland©
- March Hare Refreshments, Fantasyland©
- The Old Mill, Fantasyland©
- Studio Catering Company, All over Walt Disney Studios© Park

Help Yourself!

In lots of the restaurants you decide what you want and collect it from the counter, like in McDonald's and funnily enough there is one of them here too!

Serving delights like perfect pizzas and bonzer burgers or healthy options like sexy salads there is something for

> What do burgers think when they are surrounded by gherkins? That they are in a pickle!

everyone. All are in imaginative, kid friendly surroundings. Cheap(ish) and cheerful!

MUNCHING MUSIC

Fancy making music whilst you eat? Get everyone to rub their finger gently around their glass to make a humming noise. If you all have different amounts in the glasses you can create different notes – there you go, instant orchestral symphony!

Disneyland® Park

Fuente del Oro Restaurante

Frontierland©
Rating: ♦♦♦♦

Discover the taste of New Mexico in the funky fuente. Get stuck into tasty tacos, fab fajitas or some crazy quesadillas, scrumptious! For a

How do you make Mexican chilli?
Take him to the North Pole!

Spanish warm-you-up on a cold day try the 'churros' (long doughnuts) dipped into hot chocolate; unbeatable. Good value for money.

The Lucky Nugget Saloon

Frontierland©
Rating: ♦♦♦

Cowboy themed restaurant, but with an occasional live can-can show! This is the place to meet the Disney characters over your eat-as-much-as-you-can buffet. Gets busy during peak times so worth booking at City Hall.

Colonel Hathi's Pizza Outpost

Adventureland©
Rating: ♦♦♦

Up on stilts and hidden amongst the bamboo you'll find this mysterious pizza / pasta joint. It has an exotic and exciting atmosphere with sacred masks and

What do parrots eat when they are starving?
Polyfilla!

expedition mementoes decorating the room. Cheeky animated parrots chatter away adding to the tropical theme. It is supposed to be based on Jungle Book, not that obvious except for the music.

Restaurant Agrabah Café

Adventureland©
Rating: ♦♦♦♦

A real hidden gem, buried deep inside the Arabian bazaar. Relatively new it is lots more interesting than others. The changing menu includes exotic Mediterranean and North African nibbles; try something new! The rich and extravagant Aladdin theme creates a real sense of eastern promise. On a nice day sit outside in the courtyard. Great!

Restaurant Hakuna Matata
⌐ Adventureland©
Rating: ◈◈◈

The 'Lion King' reigns over this brightly-painted kingdom with an African theme in all of the little rooms. Noisy and busy, but that makes it more exciting. The

DID YOU KNOW?

Hakuna Matata is the Swahili words for 'no worries', 'hakuna' means 'there is no' and 'matata' is the plural of problems, so there you go. Timon and Pumbaa try to make Simba believe in 'Hakuna Matata' in the Lion King... not a bad way to approach life!

food is slightly spicy, your chicken nuggets come with Hakuna Patata spicy fries, very tasty. No worries!

Pizzeria Bella Notte
⌐ Fantasyland©
Rating: ◈◈◈

Some say this is the prettiest of the restaurants – let us know what you think.

DID YOU KNOW?

That 'Belle Notte' means 'beautiful night' in Italian.

Inspired by the "Lady and the Tramp" the décor has murals from the film as well as funny sculptures and groovy grape chandeliers. Serving simple pasta and pizzas, it is a good place to recover from 'It's a Small World' – finish off with the Tiramisu, delightful.

MORE SELF SERVICE PLACES...

- ● Market House Deli, Main Street, U.S.A.©
- ● Casey's Corner, Main Street, U.S.A.©
- ● Victoria's Home-Style Restaurant, Main Street, U.S.A.©
- ● Last Chance Cafe, Frontierland©
- ● Cowboy Cookout Barbecue, Frontierland©
- ● Toad Hall Restaurant, Fantasyland©
- ● Café Hyperion, Discoveryland©
- ● Cafe des Cascadeurs, Walt Disney Studios© Park
- ● Chuck Wagon Cafe, Disney's Hotel Cheyenne®
- ● New York Style Sandwiches, Disney® Village
- ● McDonald's®, Disney® Village

Au Chalet de la Marionnette
▣ Fantasyland©
Rating: ٥٥٥

The puppet house is a favourite with lots of visitors to the parks, but it never gets too crowded as it is really big. The food is plain and simple with lots of puddings – the place for fussy eaters.

Guests staying at the Disneyland® Hotels can have a "Good Morning Fantasyland© Breakfast", handy 'cos you get in the park early to get started on the rides.

Buzz Lightyear's Pizza Planet Restaurant
▣ Discoveryland©
Rating: ٥٥٥

Food and arcade games, a great combination. This is an exact copy of the cool pizza place in Toy Story, the one with the machine full of the cute green, bug eyed aliens. You know sometimes you can't decide between a pizza or a burger? Well here you don't have to, the speciality is a Pizzaburger, a hamburger with a mini-pizza on top!

At Disney® Hotels
Inventions
▣ Disneyland® Hotel
Rating: ٥٥٥

This restaurant is very, very nice, as you would expect in a four star hotel. The name gives the theme away, you are surrounded by 20th Century inventions. Disney Characters around for added magic (extra cost).

La Cantina
🖃 Disneys Hotel Santa Fe®
Rating: ◈◈◈
Another food court style buffet restaurant but this time the emphasis is on food from Mexico. With fabulous fajitas, brilliant burritos and tantalizing tortilla you'll be singing the cucaracha all the way home!

DID YOU KNOW?

'La Cucaracha' is a cockroach in Spanish and is the name of a famous song sung during the Mexican Revolution...

Crockett's Tavern
🖃 Disney's Davy Crockett Ranch®
Rating: ◈◈
Grab a pizza or a sizzling steak at the ho down in Davy Crockett's Tavern. It is quite bizarre – Wild West meets the Blue Lagoon as it's right next to the swimming pool! The noisy atmosphere adds to the fun, especially when the live Cowboy show is in town.

DAVID CROCKETT?

Born in 1786 this craggy frontiersman was mates with the Indians and tried to make them live happily together with the settlers, a tricky mission. Elected to the US Congress, he died a hero's death at the battle of 'The Alamo' in 1836.

At Your Service
Sometimes you deserve a special meal, for a birthday treat or a happy holiday celebration. There are some v. posh places to eat in Disneyland® Resort Paris where the surroundings, service and the scrumptious food come together for an unmissable delight. These places offer table service, just sit tight and let the magical morsels come to you!

At Disneyland® Park
Plaza Gardens Restaurant
⌨ Main Street, U.S.A.©
Rating: ♦♦♦

This is a kind of cross between a self service and table service restaurant, with velvet chairs and shiny silver knives and forks in a kind of Victorian style without being too formal. It serves a wide range of 'proper' food, things like steak, salmon etc, handy if you're fussy as you get to see what you're picking. It isn't cheap.

BIRTHDAY BONANZA!

Birthdays are very special, and they know how to celebrate them at Disneyland®! You can have your very own birthday party at the Plaza Gardens Restaurant (set price per person, currently 18 Euros) complete with a birthday cake, selection of desserts and sweets plus a surprise present just for you, often joined by Disney characters. Definitely something you'll never forget.

Walt's - an American Restaurant
⌨ Main Street, U.S.A ©
Rating: ♦♦♦

Over two floors and beautifully decorated as a tribute to both the wonderful Walt Disney and to the Parks, this is quite a place. You can eat an extravagant lunch or dinner, getting stuck into fancy fish and classic meat dishes. It is expensive, but the location and the atmosphere are special – especially good if you get a window seat when the parade is on. You can also have a character breakfast buffet here, the perfect start to a Disney® day.

Blue Lagoon Restaurant
⌨ Adventureland©
Rating: ♦♦♦♦♦

As you sail in your "Pirates of the Caribbean" boat you'll notice a really cool restaurant in the middle of the of the pirate underworld. Get a table near the

Why was Cinderella thrown off the netball team? She ran away from the ball.

69

water, 'though it's quite eerie watching people watching you eat your lunch! Serving tasty, tropical fish delights this has an interesting menu as well as the fantastic moonlit setting. The €10 Cabin boy menu with swordfish steak and a great pud is a fab deal.

Auberge de Cendrillon

☞ Fantasyland©
Rating: ♦♦♦♦♦

Cinderella's romantic restaurant is one of the best in the park. Drenched in Disney® magic the atmosphere is enchanting and the food is fancy and French. Finish with 'Cinderella's Slipper', a gorgeous concoction of white and milk chocolate mousse. Ensure you leave before midnight; it might turn into a Little Chef!

At Walt Disney Studios© Park
Backlot Express Restaurant

☞ Backlot
🕑 11am to 5.30pm
Rating: ♦♦♦

Situated in a mock Hollywood prop dump, you can grab a bite here whilst leaning on scenery from a top flick. Try out the tasty club sandwiches.

Rendez Vous des Stars Restaurant

☞ Production Courtyard
Rating: ♦♦♦♦

If you fancy yourself as a bit of a film star then

HIDE 'N' SEEK

Look out for the 'hidden Mickey' – it's above your head in the fancy mural. You can also see one of Walt's 26 Oscars.

you'll probably like it here. Stylish in an old fashioned way; you can imagine the sexy starlets taking time out in here between takes. The food is a bit more sophisticated than in other places, you can even order a birthday cake if it is your big day (extra charge).

At Disney® Hotels
These places tend to be a bit stuffy and grown up, not as much fun as the park or Disney® Village eateries. They are not bad, just not as coo-el! The two featured here score the most kid cred points.

Beaver Creek® Tavern
◻ Disney's Sequoia Lodge®
Rating: ♦♦♦
More of a happy family affair. The salad bar is tasty and big – at least you can see what you are getting. They also have a special kids desserts buffet which is very, very scrumptious!

SALAD BAR TACTICS
- Arrange cucumbers around the edge of your bowl to make it even bigger and stable.
- Check everything out before you fill your bowl, you don't want to miss the good stuff.
- Avoid boring things like lettuce.
- Remember onion gives you bad breath.
- Remember cucumber makes you burp!
- Olives are very posh and grown up - look like a gourmet...
- Keep the tomatoes until the end, pile them carefully on top.
- Leave space for lots of gooey dressing and crispy bits!

Hunter's Grill
◻ Disney's Sequoia Lodge®
Rating: ♦♦♦
Now this place has an exciting speciality – super huge kebabs on mega skewers that are carved in front of you. You can even see them being cooked in the kitchen through the glass window – coo-el.

At Disney® Village
Buffalo Bill's Wild West Show

Disney® Village
Rating: ♦♦♦♦♦

Is this a restaurant or is it a show? Who knows but it is great fun! Stick on your free cowboy hat and get stuck in to the chilli, ribs, tasty chicken, sausage and potatoes – a true cowboy feast. All whilst you are entertained by Cowboys, Indians and buffalos (yep! buffalos) in Buffalo Bill's Wild West Show. It's even better than the one in America!

TASTY TRICKS!

Try this tomato trick – ha ha !

Put a tiny slit in a cherry tomato, and hold it with the slit sideways like a mouth. Squeeze it gently at the sides so the slit opens and closes as if it's talking. Pretend it is saying something like, "Oh, I feel a bit ill, must be something I've eaten...mmm, I think I'm gonna....Uuurrrp!" On the final "Uuurp" squeeze the tomato really hard, so the crack widens and the insides spew out – good one!

Café Mickey

Disney® Village
Rating: ♦♦♦♦

This noisy, hectic kids-rule café is the place to meet the Disney characters at breakfast, lunch or dinner. Get a table by a window for a great view whilst you get stuck in to the wide selection of tasty tucker. Fab atmosphere, highly recommended, but do make a reservation.

King Ludwig's Castle

Disney® Village
Rating: ♦♦♦

The German castle setting of this place is seriously cool even if the food is not that great. Get a grown up to order the Black Knight's platter, you get 5 meats served on a sword! The best is the big puds - Black Forest Cake, very, very tasty.

Planet Hollywood®

Disney® Village
Rating: ◊◊◊◊

A groovy place to eat. Check out the famous memorobilia whilst you pig out under and around the stars. Food is fab, typical stuff that you get everywhere at Disneyland Resort Paris®, burgers, salads, yummy puddings but all very, very tasty. The service can be good, or pathetic, good luck!

Rainforest Café

Disney® Village
Rating: ◊◊◊◊

What is the difference between an elephant and a flea?
An elephant can have fleas but a flea can't have elephants!

Have you ever eaten dinner under an enormous thunderstorm whilst sitting by an elephant? Well you can do it here! Fantastic atmosphere, yummy food, seriously fun and a great ending to a fab day out at Disneyland® Resort Paris. Fancy a stuffed monkey? A cuddly one, not to eat!! You can even go shopping here, good eh?

OTHERS AT YOUR SERVICE

- Silver Spur Steakhouse, Frontierland©
- Restaurant En Coulisse, Walt Disney Studios© Park
- Annette's Diner, Disney® Village
- The Steakhouse, Disney® Village
- California Grill, Disneyland® Hotel
- Manhattan Restaurant, Disney's Hotel New York®
- Parkside Diner, Disney's Hotel New York®

Hanging Out - Shopping

Can you believe that 26 million items are sold every year in 42 shops and 23 stands in Disneyland Resort Paris®? Shopping is fun here 'cos lots of the stuff for sale is exclusive to the parks so you can't buy them anywhere else and above all some of the shops are beautiful. It is fun just wandering around!

Now shops = spending lots of money, you will easily part with the readies so be prepared. Either try to restrain yourself or save up lots of dosh.

Best Shops

There are so many shops you just won't know where to start. Here are our bonzer bazaars...

Boardwalk Candy Palace

⌐Disneyland® Park - Main Street, U.S.A.©

Sweet heaven! Giant lollipops, masses of magic, multi-coloured sweets, mouth-watering chunks of chocolate and all kinds of delights in this wonderland. Delish!

La Confiserie des Trois Fées

⌐Disneyland® Park - Fantasyland©

The three fairy's confectionary shop – how sweet... get it? They have waved their magic wands and loads of bright confections have appeared for you enjoy - yum!

Emporium

⌐ Disneyland® Park - Main Street, U.S.A.©

The biggest shop in the Disneyland® Park selling all kinds of souvenirs - some of the T-shirts are funky.

CRUCIAL COO-EL SHOPS...

- Star Traders, Discoveryland©
- Eureka Mining Supplies et Assay Office, Frontierland©
- La Boutique du Château, Fantasyland©
- Disney & Co., Main Street, U.S.A.©
- Dapper Dan's Hair Cuts, Main Street, U.S.A.©
- Rock Around the Shop, Walt Disney Studios©
- Goofy's Pro Shop, Golf Disneyland® Resort Paris

La Bottega di Geppetto

☞ Disneyland® Park - Fantasyland©

Geppetto, Pinocchio's old man's shop. Selling wicked wooden puppets, cute cuckoo clocks and magical musical boxes, for the little kids...

Legends of Hollywood,

☞ Walt Disney Studios©

It's kicking here with music and movie souvenirs.

KITSCH CLOTHES SHOPS...

- Buffalo Trading Company, Disney® Village
- Disney Clothiers, Ltd,. Main Street, U.S.A.©
- Indiana Jones™ Adventure Outpost, Adventureland©
- La Chaumière des Sept Nains, Fantasyland©
- La Girafe Curieuse, Adventureland©
- Ribbons & Bows Hat Shop, Main Street, U.S.A. ©
- Tobias Norton & Sons - Frontier Traders Frontierland©

Bonanza Outfitters

☞Disneyland Park® - Thunder Mesa Mercantile Building, Frontierland©

Why did the cowboy die with his boots on? Because he didn't want to stub his toe when he kicked the bucket!

Get your garb for the ho down from this Western Wear-house (good eh?!). Whether you're after jeans, cowboy boots a Stetson hat or natty waist-coat then you'll find it here. Woody won't be a patch on you.

DISNEY SOUVENIR SHOPS...

- The Disney Store, Main Street, U.S.A.©
- Disneyana Collectibles, Main Street, U.S.A.©
- Lilly's Boutique, Main Street, U.S.A.©
- Main Street Motors, Main Street, U.S.A.©
- Plaza West and Plaza East Boutique, Main Street, U.S.A.©
- Le Coffre du Capitaine, Adventureland©
- Merlin l'Enchanteur, Fantasyland©
- Constellations, Discoveryland©
- Walt Disney Studios Store , Walt Disney Studios©
- The Disney Animation Gallery, Walt Disney Studios©
- Art Gallery, Disney® Village
- Hollywood Pictures, Disney® Village
- Galerie Mickey, Disneyland® Hotel
- New York Boutique, Disney's Hotel New York®
- Bay Boutique, Disney's Newport Bay Club®
- Northwest Passage, Disney's Sequoia Lodge®
- General Store, Disney's Hotel Cheyenne®
- Trading Post, Disney's Hotel Santa Fe®

Les Trésors de Schéhérazade

Disneyland® Park - Adventureland©
Get your mitts on Sheherezad's Treasures from far-off
lands found during the voyages of Sinbad the Sailor.

TIP TOP TOY SHOPS...

- La Petite Maison des Jouets, Fantasyland©
- La Ménagerie du Royaume, Fantasyland©
- Le Brave Petit Tailleur, Fantasyland©
- World Of Toys, Disney® Village

Handy Shops

Town Square Photography

Disneyland® Park - Main Street, U.S.A.©
Where you can buy or rent cameras, video cameras
etc. and they have a 2-hour developing service.

La Poste
📭 Disney® Village

The Post Office is at the Marne la Vallée train station.

Bureau De Change
📭 Disney® Village

Where you change your hard earned dosh into euros.

Hanging Out - Back To Nature

You don't really come to Disneyland® Resort Paris for the animals or the landscapes do you? But if you are a nature lover check these out...

Disneyland® Park

Critter Corral
📭 Frontierland©
① ☇
Rating: ₰

Cheeky chickens from Critter Corral greet you at Frontierland Station. They really are free range, roaming about pecking everything in their way. Critter Corral is

> Why did the chicken cross the road, roll in the mud and cross the road again?
> Because he was a dirty double-crosser!

also home to ducks, rabbits, donkeys and sheep. Wander amongst them and give them a cuddle. More for little kiddies.

Thunder Mesa Riverboat Landing
📭 Frontierland©
① ☇ ₰ (Lasts 15 mins)
Rating: ₰₰₰

If you want a change of pace after running madly around the park, then this is perfect. Two paddle boats "Mark Twain" and Molly

Brown" meander around Big Thunder Mountain. Look

out for the steaming Geyser Plateau (based on the natural geysers in Yellowstone National Park) which shoots up jets of water. See if you can spot the dinosaur bones, thought they were extinct...

La Cabane Des Robinson
(The Swiss Family Robinson Treehouse)
Discoveryland©
ⓘ ♒
Rating: ◔◔

Trek up the intrepid staircase into the wild and wobbly driftwood Treehouse created by the shipwrecked Robinson family. Not hugely exciting but you do get a good view! Explore the roots of the tree, an amazing maze of passageways

CRAZY CABANE FACTS

The fascinating fig tree has:
- Over 360,000 handmade leaves
- Over 130,000 blooms

And is over 28 metres high!

awaits, the 'Ventre de la Terre' ('stomach of the earth' – hope it doesn't rumble down there!).

Adventure Isle
Discoveryland©
ⓘ ♒
Rating: ◔◔◔

Explore and live out your fantasies of being an intrepid explorer on a death defying expedition on Adventure Isle. The best bits are Skull Rock (when it gets dark) with the groaning skeleton beneath; Captain Hook's Pirate Ship (a bit babyish) and the rickety

rope bridge – some scaredy cats get really petrified on this – jumping up and down on it is not a nice thing to do (but is realllllllly funny!). Ben Gunn's caves are good for game of hide and seek.

Hanging Out - Being Sporty

Doing sport is not the main reason that you'll be going to Disneyland® Resort Paris but if you are super sporty then you might want to know what is there to satisfy your cravings!

Football
Manchester United Soccer School (MUSS)

✉ Training Camp by Disney's Sequoia Lodge® and Newport Bay Hotel®
ⓘ   Costs €25 - 2½ hour session
Rating: ♦♦♦♦

The most exciting sporting activity is the new Manchester United Soccer School (MUSS) coaching programme. Developed by Manchester United's Youth Academy, the starting ground of Becks, Giggs and Scholes, it is an unforgettable experience. You are coached by UEFA/FA qualified coaches focusing on the key elements of football, like dribbling, passing, tackling and shooting.   It is not just for football supremos, it is for 7-14 year old boys _and_ girls at all levels of experience and playing ability. Don't forget your sports gear and shower kit if this is your kind of thing.

NOTE: Availability may be restricted – check for eligibility and availability at the Information Desk.

Pony Rides
Davy Crockett's Pony Rides

✉ Disney's Davy Crockett Ranch Farm®
ⓘ Cost varies
Rating: ♦♦

On a sunny day what can be nicer than a little trot around the paddock on a friendly pony? Get on down to the Davy Crockett Ranch Farm for a little trek, it does cost a bit extra but it is worth it.

Golf

Disneyland® Paris Golf Club
⌐ 1 Allee de la Marc Houleuse, 77400 Magny-le-Hongre
☎ (0) 60 45 68 04
ⓘ Open daily, all year round   Cost varies (from €3.50 for 30 driving
range balls to over €50 to play)

Rating: ♦♦♦

If you are a golf superstar head on down to Disney's
very own golf course. With three 9 hole golf courses,
2 biggies that combine together to make a proper
6032m, Par 72, 18 hole course plus a smaller 9 hole
golf course, all suitable for players of all abilities.
There is also a pitching and putting green for practis-
ing. Not <u>especially</u> for kids, but you can play.

Ice Skating

⌐ Disney's Hotel New York® Ice Skating Rink
ⓘ ☺ ☾November-End March   Costs €7 kids (€10 adults -€2 if you have
own skates)
Rating: ♦♦♦

If you are going to Disneyland Resort Paris® during
the winter then try to find time for a spot of ice
skating. Directly in front of Disney's Hotel New York®
and by the lake is the artificial ice rink. Not the biggest
in the world but big enough to practise your turns or
try a bit of speed skating and it's not always that busy.

Swimming

Most of the Disney® Hotels have swimming
pools as does Davy Crockett's Ranch®, so
if you are staying in one of them you can
swim every day. Watch out, Disney's
Hotel Santa Fe® and Disney's Hotel Cheyenne® do not
have swimming facilities. Lots of other Hotels nearby
also have pools.

Hanging Out - Not So Far Away

Not only is there masses to do at the Disneyland®
Resort Paris ; you've got fantastic shopping and a

Sea Life Centre nearby and Paris is only a short hop on the train (well maybe a longish hop, not far away!).

We've not got a lot of space left in the book (and it is supposed to be about Disneyland® Resort Paris) so we're going to have to cover these off in a short, sharp fashion – the essential essentials.

Val D'Europe

Val D'Europe Shopping Centre

☉ Open 7 days a week, 10am-7pm (11am on Sundays, 8pm in summer)
🖳 www.valdeurope.fr

When you want a quick escape from all things Disney® then hop on the RER A4 train or on the shuttle bus to the chic shopping centre at Val D'Europe. Less than 10 minutes away, pop over for lunch or an early dinner. It's a must place to go at the end of your hols to spend those left over euros!

> **TOP 5 SHOPS IN VAL D'EUROPE**
> - Tommy Hilfiger
> - Reebok
> - Miss Sixty
> - Pimkie
> - Ben & Jerry's

Sea Life Centre

📠 Espace 502, 14, Cours Du Danube – Serris 77711, Marne La Vallee
☎ (0)1 60 42 33 66
☉ Open 7 days a week, from 10am-5.30pm
🖳 www.sealifeeurope.com

If you like all things fishy, head down to the Sea Life Centre Aquarium for a thrilling shark attack and cracking crusty crustaceans (shellfish to you and me!). It's more hard core than 'Nemo', with real sharks, rays and a super-size skate swimming right above your head in huge sea-like tanks.
You can even touch a ray – coo-el!

> **DID YOU KNOW?**
> Giant spider crabs in southern Japan are HUGE! A full grown male can reach one and a half metres in height and will span about four metres – big enough to cover a whole car. Hope you don't ever meet one...

Paris

There are millions of things to do in the Paris area (seek out the science museum, go mad in the Asterix Park, ride a bike in the Bois de Boulogne, go to the Zoo, swim at the Aqua Boulevard, visit Versailles…. phew!) ask at the Tourist Info if any of this takes your fancy.

PARIS TOP 5

- Eiffel Tower
- L'Arc De Triomphe / Champs Elysées
- Le Louvre
- Cathédrales de Notre Dame
- Sacre Coeur / Montmartre

Getting Around

Public Transport

Paris has a great transport system with the metro, the RER, buses and it is a city you can easily walk around.

If you are planning a day out exploring then it is worth buying a 'Paris Visite' card from any metro or train station. This gives you unlimited rides within the Île-de-France region on the Metro, RER, bus, tramway, suburban Transilien SNCF trains, the funicular railway at Montmartre, Montmartrobus, Noctambus and the Optile bus system, within a given fare zone (from 1-3, 1-5 to 1-8). This includes Disneyland® Resort Paris (zone 5, about 40 minutes from the city centre).

A 1 day pass costs €8.35 for kids and €16.75 for adults and also gives you a few deals at museums and some shops (including at Disneyland® Resort Paris).

Check out 🖳 www.parisvisite.tm.fr/english for the latest info.

Coach Tour

ⓘ Daily 9.45am – 6.30pm   Costs €31 kids (€61 adults + over 12's)
Evening Tour 8pm – Midnight   Costs €12 kids (€42 adults + over 12's)

Cityrama run coach tours of Paris directly from Disneyland® Resort Paris, picking up from outside Disney's Hotel New York®. This is the easiest way to see the city, covering most of the main sites and including a boat ride up the Seine, English speaking info and a trip to the first floor of the Eiffel Tower.

There are also toilets on board – very handy. However it isn't the cheapest, the most flexible or the most exciting. You do get some time to yourself at lunch to wander around Notre Dame or grab a quick crepe in the Latin Quarter but you get shepherded around apart from that.

An extra special treat is seeing Paris, the 'city of lights' at night time. The evening tour is very late, but worth staying up for if you can last until midnight.

Tourist Info.

The Tourist Office at the Marne la Vallée station has lots of info. about the things to do in the city of Paris. Pop in before you head to the big smoke. If you forget there is another in the city centre.

Check out :
🖥 www.paris-ile-de-france.com and
🖥 www.parisbienvenue.com
☎ (0) 892 68 31 12

DID YOU KNOW?

On some Sundays the museums in Paris are free – ask for details at the Tourist info office. Other places are always free for kids (Musée D'Orsay / Musée Picasso)!

THE Places to See / Things to Do

L'Arc de Triomphe / Champs Elysées

📭 Place du Général de Gaulle, Paris 75008
☎ (0) 55 37 73 77
Tube / Station Charles-de Gaulle-Etoile
⏲ Open Daily 9.30am-11pm (seasonal variations) Costs €7

Walk up the 284 steps for a great Parisian view, including the Eiffel Tower. L'Arc de Triomphe is the biggest

triumphal arch in the world, commissioned in 1806 by little Napoleon Bonaparte to commemorate the French Army's victories. At the top of the café and shopping paradise of the Champs Elysées, it's a great place to start a tour of Paris.

Bateaux Parisiens

⌐ Seine under the Eiffel Tower
☎ (0) 1 44 11 33 44
Tube / Station Champ de Mars
☺ Open Daily, every 30 mins 10am-11pm (10pm, hourly in low season)
Costs €4.1 kids (€9 adults + over 12's)
⌨ www.bateauxparisiens.com

Bateaux Mouche

⌐ Port de la conférence, Pont de l'Alma, Rive droite, Paris 75008
☎ (0) 1 44 11 33 44 / 1 40 76 99 99   Tube / Station Pont de l'Alma
☺ Open Daily, every 30 mins 10am-8pm (specific times in low season)
Costs €4 kids (€7 adults + over 12's)
⌨ www.bateaux-mouches.fr

A fantastic way to see some of the main sights of Paris is from a boat riding along the Seine. Two groups of boats do sightseeing tours, the Bateaux Mouche and the Bateaux Parisiens, both offer a great experience especially on a bright sunny day or in the evening when you see the bright twinkling lights of Paris.

Cathédrale de Notre Dame

⌐ Place du Parvis de Notre-Dame, Paris 75001
☎ (0) 1 42 34 56 10
Tube / Station Saint Michel-Notre Dame, Cité
☺ Open Daily 8 am -6.45 pm Costs €7

DID YOU KNOW?

All road distances in France are calculated from the "0 km" sign marked in front of the cathedral.

This big old cathedral was build between 1163 and 1345, builders took a long time in those days too! You might recognise it from Quasimodo's movie although the Hunchback is nowhere to be seen. Nice gardens outside!

Eiffel Tower

⌐ Champs-de-Mars, Paris 75007
☎ (0) 1 44 11 23 23
Tube / Station Champ de Mars-Tour Eiffel
☺ Open Daily 9.30am to 6.30pm (stairs open until midnight)
Costs €5.70 kids (€10.70 adults, less if you use stairs)
⌨ www.tour-eiffel.fr

You can't go to Paris without seeing Gustave Eiffel's tottering tower; it is even more amazing in real life - honest. Completed in 1889, it was at the time the tallest tower in the whole world. You can go up to three floors, the first at 57 m., the second at 115m., and the third at 276 m. However the top of the aerial is a huge 320 m. above the ground. If it's a sunny day you can see the whole of Paris and even the distant suburbs – maybe even Disneyland® Resort Paris.

Musée du Louvre

Palais du Louvre, Cours Napoléon, Paris 75001
☎ (0) 55 37 73 77
Tube / Station Palais-Royal, Louvre
🕐 Open Daily 9am-6 pm (10pm Mon & Weds, Closed Tuesday)
Costs €7
🖳 www.louvre.fr

Go into the Louvre through Carrousel du Louvre mall on rue de Rivoli entrance, it's much faster to enter than through the pyramid.

This is one of the grooviest art galleries ever. The best bit is the huge glass pyramid that covers one of the

entrances, quite stunning. It is home to the miserable 'Mona Lisa', Van Gogh's jazzy 'Sunflowers' and the mystical 'Venus de Milo' statue.

Did you hear the Mona Lisa was brought up in court on charges of murder? It turned out that she'd been framed. Tee hee!

Pompidou Art Center

Rue du Renard, Paris 75004
☎ (0) 44 78 12 33   Tube / Station Hôtel-de-Ville, Rambuteau, Châtelet
🕐 Open Daily from 11am-10pm except Tuesdays
Costs €8 kids (€10 adults)
🖳 www.centrepompidou.fr

This is a kind of modern culture centre where you can watch arty films, see funky exhibitions, find out about revolutionary books or see a thought provoking play. It was the brain child of George Pompidou, an art guru. They hold special children's activities, check out the website for details. It is worth going just to see the funky futuristic building and having a ride in the groovy lifts! At night time it lights up and looks amazing.

Sacre Coeur / Montmartre

Parvis du Sacré-Coeur, Paris 75018
☎ (0) 53 41 89 00
Tube / Station Anvers
⏲ Open Daily Basilica 6am-11pm / Dôme 9am-5.30pm (7pm in summer)
Costs €free (Dôme €5)
🖳 www.sacre-coeur-montmartre.com

This is one of those wow places, beautiful to look at and fantastic to look from. The basilica is beautiful and tranquil, but the outside is where it is at. In the summer you can dip your toes in the lovely fountains and all year round you can watch the artists that gather in Montmartre. This is where the famous Impressionist Painters used to hang out. Don't miss out on the vertical funicular railway (included in the Paris Visite card) - views while you are elevated! Well worth the metro ride.

Wonder Wander

If you are a free and easy, dreamy kind of traveller then just go for a wander. Paris is one of those cities where you can simply stroll around and take in the sights, discovering your own favourite places.

If this is more your thing then start at L'Arc De Triomphe at the top of the Champs Elysées and wander down towards the majestic Place de la Concorde and along the Quai des Tuilleries to the Louvre (a long but inter-

Check out the rollerbladers around the Eiffel Tower - some of them are really cool.

esting walk). A little further on is the Pont Neuf where you can cross the Seine to the Left Bank, taking in Notre Dame. The Left Bank is home to the 'Quartier Latin' (Latin Quarter) where all the trendy students hang out and you can grab cheap eats here – the crêpes are highly recommended.

Then grab the RER C towards Versailles / La Défense and get off at Champs De Mars (Tour Eiffel) to see the elevating Eiffel Tower. If you feel energetic then climb up to stairs for a great view, other wise take the lift or just wander around, it's quite chilled around here.

Finally grab a Bateau Mouche or a Bateau Parisien back the river down towards Notre Dame. A great end to a day wandering Paris!

.

Can't be bothered to read the whole book? Want it all laid out on one page that is easy to follow? Good job we've done these day planners then!

We have included the MUST DO rides and suggested shows/events that will make your days sooper dooper. We can't be exactly precise about what time to do things as times change and you need to be flexible to allow for queueing. Check these out when you arrive in the Parks.

We'd love to hear your comments about what you think of the Ultimate days, do you agree with them... like to suggest something else...? Then drop us an email at hello@knapsackguides.com.

The Ultimate Day Out - Disneyland® Park

Start early to fit everything in, get in as soon as the park opens. Go to your favourite ride first thing in the morning and save the other biggies for lunch time (1pm-2pm) and parade time - use Fastpass where poss. Do repeat runs after you've done everything else you want.

We recommend seeing the parades and shows too., they are what Disney is all about!

The Ultimate Day Out - Walt Disney Studios© Park

Same advice as for Disneyland® Park - get in early and do biggies first. This park is smaller so you should find it a lot easier to get around everything.

There are only two Fastpass rides, get Fastpasses for them first and then head off to the other rides.

Finish off with a spot of shopping and dinner in the Rainforest Café. Two great Ultimate days.

Day Planner Timed Attractions/Must Do's - Disneyland Park

What	Where	Start	Finish
Mickey's Show Time	Discoveryland©	am (check times on arrival)	Show approx 30mins
The Chaparral Theater	Frontierland©	pm (check times on arrival)	Show approx 25mins
Princes Parade	Main St USA©	4pm	30mins to pass by
Disney's Fantillusion	Main St USA©	After 7.30pm (check times)	30mins to pass by
Fireworks	Sleeping Beauty Castle	Seasonal (check if on)	Approx 10mins

What	Where	Notes	
Big Thunder Mountain	Frontierland©	Ride a runaway train (Fastpass if busy).	
Phantom Manor	Frontierland©	Haunted by 999 ghosts, enter if you dare...	
Indiana Jones™ (Temple of Peril:Backwards)	Adventureland©	Hurtle backwards through an old temple, oh yes!	
Pirates of the Caribbean	Adventureland©	Yo ho ho and a bottle of rum, party with pirates!	
Space Mountain	Discoveryland©	Get blasted into space by a big gun, great fun.	
Star Tours	Discoveryland©	Take part in your own 'Star Wars' adventure.	
Honey, I Shrunk the Audience	Discoveryland©	Get shrunk, that's just the start of the surprises.	

Day Planner Timed Attractions/Must Do's - Walt Disney Studios© Park

What	Where	Start	Finish
Cinemagique	Production Courtyard	10.30am	10.55am
Animagique®	Animation Courtyard	11.30am	11.50am
Disney® Cinema Parade	All over the park!	1.45pm	Approx 2.15pm
Moteurs ... Action! Stunt Show®	Backlot!	3.15pm (arrive 30mins early)	4.20pm

What	Where	Notes	
Rock 'n' Roller Coaster	Backlot	Have to do this at least once, best ride in the park.	
Studio Tram Tour®	Production Courtyard	See behind the magic, it's hot stuff!	
Television Production Tour	Production Courtyard	See TV Tricks, great cybercoaster ride at the end.	
Flying Carpets over Agrabah®	Animation Courtyard	Get onto a magic carpet. If busy Fastpass it.	
Armageddon	Backlot	Only if there is no queue and there is nothing else...	

In the evening you can get into the Disneyland® Park with your Studio's ticket (3 hrs before closing) - yippee!

HANDY STUFF

Childline – free 24hr   0800 1111
NSPCC Child Protection Helpline 0808 800 5000

Emergencies
Medical / Ambulance   15
Police / Gendarmarie   17
Fire   18
Pan European (also mobile emergency no.)   112

British Embassy
⌐ 5 rue du Faubourg St Honoré, 75383 Paris
☎ (1) 44 51 31 00
🖳 www.amb-grandebretagne.fr

Disney® Information
🖳 www.disneylandparis.com
Disneyland Paris Guest Relations
⌐ Boite Postale 100, F-77777 Marne-la-Vallée, Cédex 4, France
☎ (1) 60 30 60 30
🖳 email: message_edl-admin@dlp.disney.com

🖳 www.dlp-guidebook.de
🖳 www.dlrpfans.be
🖳 www.solarius.com/dvp/dlp
🖳 www.dlpfoodguide.com

Don't forget to get lots of brochures from your local travel agents,
they tell you what they think of the place and you'll see lots of
photos.

Cash Points (handy places to take your parents...)
⌐ Disneyland® Park, in the arcades parallel to Main Street,
U.S.A., Discoveryland and Adventureland
⌐Walt Disney Studios® Park, next to Studio Services and at the
Backlot Express Restaurant.
⌐ At the Post Office in Marne-la-Vallée/Chessy station.
⌐ At the Gaumont Cineplex in Disney® Village.
⌐ At the Convention Centre in Disney's Newport Bay Club.

Post Boxes
There are several yellow post boxes in the Parks. Post is taken to
the Post Office every day by the Cast Members. Stamps are on
sale in the Disneyland® Resort Paris shops

Tourist Information
- Tourist Information Centre, Marne-la-Vallée Station
- Paris Convention and Visitors Bureau, 127 avenue des Champs-Elysées, 75008 Paris
- ☎ (1) 49 52 53 54 / 56

- www.paris-tourist-information.com
- www.123paris.net/kids-paris.html
- www.paris-tourism.com/kids/
- www.discover-paris.info

Transport
Public transport for Paris and its suburbs.
- www.ratp.fr
- www.ratp.fr/ParisVisite/Eng/index.htm

Paris Visite Travel / Discount Pass
- www.parisvisite.tm.fr/english

Cityrama Coach Tours
- www.cityrama.com/sightseeing.html
Pick up Info. at Disneyland Resort Paris® Hotels or Tourist Information Centre

Airports
Orly Aiport
☎ (1) 49 75 15 15
Paris Charles de Gaulle Airport
☎ (1) 48 62 22 80

- www.adp.fr/webadp/a_cont01_an.nsf/NFhome@ReadForm.html
Airport Shuttle Buses : http://paris.shuttle-airport.com

Ferries
www.seafrance.co.uk
www.posl.com

Learning French
- http://funschool.com/
- http://library.thinkquest.org/18783/funfrench.html

FINALLY BUT MOST IMPORTANTLY!!!
- www.knapsackguides.com
- Knapsack Publishing Ltd., The Beach Hut, PO Box 124, Hove. BN3 3JP
- ☎ 01273 737276